AF477276

# AI-POWERED SECURE SOFTWARE ENGINEERING

Preventing Financial Fraud Through Cybersecurity & AI

Gbenga Akingbulere

ISBN: 978-625-447-436-1

Published in Nigeria
Prodigy Press

A catalogue record of this book will be available from the National Library of Nigeria.

# TABLE OF CONTENTs

# Preface

When I started out in software engineering, cybersecurity felt like a specialized field, something left to dedicated teams, tucked away behind the backend logic and user interfaces most of us focused on. But things changed quickly. The systems we built were suddenly handling more data, more money, and more responsibility than ever before. And before long, one thing became clear: if you're building software especially in finance, you're also building security, whether you plan to or not.

This book is a direct response to that shift.

Over the last few years, I've been deeply involved in engineering financial systems that don't just function but protect. Platforms where fraud detection happens in milliseconds. Systems that can flag anomalies, trigger alerts, and even respond to threats without waiting for human intervention. Along the way, I've worked with brilliant teams, built and rebuilt architectures, and seen firsthand how even small oversights in design can become major risks at scale.

And one thing I've learned? Security can no longer be an afterthought. It must be part of how we design, build, and deploy software from the very beginning.

This book exists because financial platforms don't have the luxury of catching up anymore. The threats are fast. The damage is expensive. And users, regulators, and businesses all expect that security is already baked into what they're using.

But here's the thing: secure software is possible, when it's intentional. That's where AI comes in. Not as a buzzword or band-aid, but as a tool for building smarter systems that learn, adapt, and scale. AI gives us a real opportunity to shift from reactive to proactive from fixing issues after a breach, to preventing them before they happen.

Throughout these chapters, I'll share what I've learned about using AI and sound engineering practices to build enterprise-grade financial security applications. We'll explore how to design fraud detection models that work in production, not just in theory. We'll break down real-world use cases where AI helped us identify risks earlier, reduce false positives, and respond faster. And we'll talk through the structural decisions that matter when you're building cloud-native, scalable, and secure systems that actually hold up under pressure.

This isn't just a book for engineers. It's for software professionals, security specialists, DevOps teams, and fintech leaders, anyone involved in designing, building, maintaining, or scaling financial software. The examples I share are grounded in real challenges from the field: conflicting priorities, technical debt, team constraints, and evolving threat landscapes. This is the side of software security that doesn't always make it into documentation but shows up daily in practice.

You'll find each chapter structured around a clear goal. First, we'll set the context; what problem are we solving? Then, we'll explore practical principles, architectural patterns, and implementation techniques that support that goal. And finally, where relevant, I'll walk through real-world scenarios or decisions I've encountered, successes and mistakes alike.

This is also not a book that assumes a single way of doing things. Engineering, especially in security, is filled with trade-offs. You'll need to adapt based on your environment, your stack, your team, and your users. My aim is to offer a flexible, reliable foundation, one that helps you ask the right questions, make more informed decisions, and build with clarity.

Lastly, this book is a product of collaboration. The insights shared here were shaped by experiences with colleagues, mentors, and even competitors. From reviewing software submissions and judging research papers, to leading internal reviews of fraud detection engines, I've had the privilege of seeing this work from multiple angles. That perspective helped shape the practical lens this book is written through.

If you take away anything from this book, let it be this: security is not separate from software; it is software. And when we bring security into our architecture, when we build with learning systems in mind, and when we align our tools with real-world risk, we build platforms people can actually trust.

Thank you for reading. I hope this book supports your work and helps you think more deeply about how we design systems that not only work but protect what matters.

Let's get to it.

# Foreword

In today's financial landscape, security is no longer a support function, it is the infrastructure. The systems that carry transactions, manage identities, and protect sensitive data must be intelligent, scalable, and secure by default. But building those systems requires more than just technical expertise. It demands clarity, consistency, and a deep understanding of how evolving threats interact with complex software ecosystems.

That's where Gbenga Akingbulere's work stands out.

I've followed Gbenga's career closely from his early days working on core financial systems to his later contributions in AI-powered fraud detection and cybersecurity automation. What's impressed me most is not just the depth of his knowledge, but the way he applies it. He doesn't chase trends. He builds intentionally, combining strong engineering foundations with emerging technologies in ways that actually work.

This book is a reflection of that discipline.

In *AI-Powered Secure Software Engineering: Preventing Financial Fraud Through Cybersecurity & AI*, Gbenga breaks down what many in our industry often overcomplicate. He shows how software engineers, DevSecOps teams, and fintech professionals can apply practical principles to solve real security problems without relying on hype or theory.

From designing fraud detection systems that run in production, to understanding how to scale cloud-native applications securely, this book offers clarity where most only offer surface-level explanation. More importantly, it focuses on how to build responsibly, how to align automation with accountability, and how to embed intelligence without weakening control.

If you work in software, finance, or security, this book will push you to think differently. It won't hand you shortcuts. But it will give you the tools and perspective to design systems that protect as much as they perform.

Gbenga Akingbulere has done more than write about best practices, he's lived them. I have no doubt that this book will become a trusted reference for teams building the next generation of secure financial systems.

**_Ignatius Nmakwe, MBA, PMP, CSCMP_**

# Introduction

We live in a time where financial systems are under more pressure than ever. Not just to work, but to withstand, to adapt, and to defend. The push toward digital transformation has been swift and necessary, but it has also introduced a level of complexity that traditional software engineering principles can no longer manage alone. In a landscape where fraud evolves daily and attackers constantly probe for weaknesses, the software that powers finance must do more than function; it must learn, respond, and protect in real time.

This book was written to meet that need.

As someone who's worked at the intersection of software engineering and financial security for several years, I've come to believe that the way we build systems needs to change. We can't keep patching vulnerabilities into security strategies or waiting for post-incident investigations to improve our response. We have to engineer software with security as a first principle, not a final step. And in today's world, that also means leaning on artificial intelligence as a core part of the solution.

But AI is not a magic bullet. It's only as good as the context, data, and design that frame it. This book isn't about promoting AI for the sake of buzzwords. It's about understanding what AI can actually do in the realm of secure financial software and how to use it responsibly.

We'll explore what it takes to build intelligent fraud detection systems that work in production not just in prototypes. We'll look at how cloud-native security infrastructures can be used to scale defense across regions. We'll break down DevSecOps practices, not just as a philosophy, but as a repeatable set of actions that help prevent late-stage security bottlenecks. And we'll examine real systems, drawn from actual financial use cases, that show how secure software should be designed in the real world, under real conditions, with real consequences.

This book is written with practitioners in mind. If you're a software engineer who's ever had to choose between shipping fast and building safely, or a security professional trying to embed protection into a CI/CD pipeline without slowing down development, this book is for you. If you're leading a team inside a fintech company and need to think through how to scale safely without overcomplicating your stack, you'll find clarity here. And if you're working in banking or cybersecurity; building, reviewing, or auditing software that must meet regulatory expectations while still delivering on user demands, this book was written with your world in mind.

You won't find one-size-fits-all solutions here. Secure software is contextual. What works for a large-scale mobile payments platform may not apply to a traditional banking backend. But the principles, strategies, and frameworks shared in these pages are adaptable. They are grounded in experience and drawn from working systems not theory.

You'll find discussions around how to build AI systems that improve over time, without introducing bias or unnecessary complexity. You'll see how to structure fraud detection layers into your application stack so that they complement your infrastructure instead of slowing it down. We'll talk about how to prepare for the auditability and transparency challenges that come with using AI in decision-making systems. And importantly, we'll explore what to do when systems fail, because resilience is just as important as prevention.

There's also an emphasis in this book on the collaborative nature of building secure systems. Security is not a task reserved for a single role or team. It touches frontend and backend, infrastructure and business logic, design and deployment. Throughout these chapters, I'll highlight how development, operations, and security must work together, technically and culturally to deliver systems that scale and protect at the same time.

What makes financial systems unique is that they demand real-time accuracy, trust, and performance. A delay in fraud detection is not just a bug, it can be a breach. A poor architectural decision can result in cascading risks that impact thousands or millions of users. That's why this book focuses so heavily on software engineering as the core because the systems we're protecting are only as strong as the decisions we make during design and development.

You'll also find case studies drawn from enterprise systems that have been deployed, tested, and evolved in real financial environments. These stories reflect the challenges that often don't show up in formal documentation, what it takes to scale AI without bloating infrastructure, how teams handle conflicting priorities between speed and safety, and how systems respond when the threat isn't a known exploit, but a behavioral anomaly hiding in plain sight.

There's no single playbook for secure software engineering in finance, but there is a path. A way to approach problems with clarity. A way to build without fear that you're introducing more risk than you're solving. A way to use AI not just because it's available, but because it genuinely improves how your system sees, learns, and reacts.

This book is structured to guide you through that path, starting with the foundational principles of secure software engineering, moving into how AI can be applied effectively in cybersecurity, and then diving into infrastructure, automation, ethics, and the future of intelligent systems. Each chapter builds on the one before it, but you can also read them as standalones, depending on what you're working on or solving for right now.

As engineers and architects, we don't just shape software, we shape systems people rely on. In finance, that means protecting livelihoods, transactions, and trust. The goal isn't to scare developers into taking security seriously, it's to empower them to build systems that are intelligent, resilient, and trustworthy by design.

This is not a theoretical book. It's not a shallow overview. It's a field-tested guide for software professionals who care about building well and building secure.

If that's you, then let's get started.

# Reviews

### Adanna Chukwuma

*Software Engineer, Lagos*

*"This book doesn't romanticize AI, it treats it like a tool that needs structure, context, and accountability. As someone actively working on backend systems in fintech, I found the insights on AI-powered fraud detection especially useful. Gbenga breaks down the complexity without watering it down. It's the kind of book I wish I had when I started working on financial APIs."*

### Tolu Adebayo

*Cybersecurity Analyst, Abuja*

*"Practical, focused, and long overdue. Too many conversations about cybersecurity stay at the surface level. What Gbenga has done here is impressive, he connects engineering principles with real-world fraud patterns and shows how AI can support, not replace decision-making. This book deserves a spot on every DevSecOps shelf."*

### Ifeanyi Eze

*CTO, Mid-size Fintech Startup, Enugu*

*"Gbenga Akingbulere has written the kind of book we need more of in the Nigerian tech ecosystem, grounded in local experience but global in relevance. The case studies hit home because they mirror the challenges we face every day, scaling securely, handling fraud in real time, and working with lean teams. Every engineering lead in fintech should read this."*

## Hafsat Lawal

*DevOps Engineer, Kaduna*

*"This book bridges a knowledge gap I didn't know how to articulate. Most security resources talk about principles. This one show how to implement them, through CI/CD, cloud-native tools, and team workflows. It's especially helpful for engineers looking to embed security into fast-moving product teams without slowing them down."*

## Chidi Okonkwo

*AI Researcher & Technical Reviewer, Port Harcourt*

*"What stood out to me was Gbenga's ability to balance AI theory with deployment realities. The book isn't just for engineers, it's for reviewers, security consultants, and even compliance professionals who want to understand how these systems work under the hood. It's rare to find something this readable that still goes this deep."*

# CHAPTER ONE
## The Evolving Threat Landscape in Financial Software

It doesn't take a breach to know that a system is vulnerable. Sometimes the signs are subtle, a strange sequence of logins from unfamiliar locations, a slight delay in transaction processing, or an unusual spike in user activity during odd hours. In today's financial ecosystem, these small signals often point to something deeper. The line between routine behavior and malicious activity has grown thinner, and it is in these grey areas that modern fraud thrives. What makes the situation even more complex is the fact that financial services, more than most industries, are in a state of constant digital acceleration. Mobile banking, instant transfers, digital wallets, blockchain-backed platforms, open APIs, these innovations have redefined convenience and access. But they have also expanded the surface area for potential attacks, often faster than security teams can adapt.

Financial software isn't just being asked to scale anymore. It's being asked to protect. Threat actors today aren't guessing passwords or defacing websites, they are reverse-engineering APIs, deploying intelligent bots, social engineering support staff, and using AI to study the behavior of both users and systems. Many operate like product teams: they run simulations, test scenarios, and refine their tactics continuously. The unfortunate truth is that they are often more agile than the systems they're targeting. And that's where engineering has to evolve. Security in this context is not simply a matter of patching known vulnerabilities or deploying firewalls. It requires an approach that begins at the level of design, architecting systems that understand behavior, monitor change, and respond in real time with minimal human involvement.

For a long time, financial software relied heavily on static security rules. If a transaction exceeded a threshold, it was flagged. If login attempts failed repeatedly, the account was locked. If an IP address was blacklisted, access was denied. These systems were predictable and easy to maintain. But they were just as easy to study and bypass. Attackers could test the limits, learn the rules, and evolve faster than the protections. In today's landscape, where digital systems must process thousands of transactions per second and serve millions of users across geographies, this approach no longer holds.

This is where artificial intelligence begins to play a crucial role. AI, when applied responsibly, can enable systems to move from reactive to proactive. It allows platforms to learn from patterns, flag inconsistencies, and act without waiting for someone to interpret the data. Imagine a user whose behavior over time shows a pattern of local transactions during weekday mornings. One night, a high-value transfer request is made to a foreign account from a new device. A rules-based system might pass it through if it technically doesn't violate any single condition. But an AI-powered system, trained on behavioral patterns and transaction contexts, might see that the request breaks from expected behavior. It might notice recent failed login attempts, a device change, or other subtle signals that, when combined, raise the risk score. Such a system could pause the transaction, escalate it, or trigger further checks, all before any funds move.

The shift from rigid rule sets to adaptive intelligence is not just a technological upgrade, it's a necessity. The cost of fraud, both financial and reputational, is rising. A single breach can lead to millions in losses, not to mention regulatory penalties and erosion of customer trust. For organizations that build or manage financial platforms, the expectations have changed. Users expect that their money is secure, that suspicious activity is caught early, and that systems don't fail when it matters most. Yet, many engineering teams still treat security as a task to be completed after launch. This mindset is not only outdated, it is dangerous.

Secure software engineering in the financial sector is no longer optional. It is foundational. And it starts with recognizing that security is not a function separate from development, it is a core part of how systems are architected. This means designing infrastructure with security boundaries, building APIs with abuse in mind, embedding logging and monitoring into every layer, and assuming that failure will happen at some point. It also means understanding trade-offs where performance can be balanced with protection, and where user experience must not be compromised in the name of control.

This is where many systems fail quietly. They're designed to perform, not to evolve. Codebases become rigid. Security checks are bolted on rather than embedded. Logging is treated as a burden rather than a tool. And worst of all, teams operate in silos, security reviewing after development, operations scrambling after deployment, and compliance showing up only when a regulator asks for documentation. This fractured model can no longer hold up under the demands of today's financial software environment.

Instead, we must embrace security as a layered responsibility. Engineers need to write code with threat modeling in mind, not just performance optimization. Product teams must understand how design decisions influence user behavior and potential misuse. Security professionals must work alongside developers to evaluate tools, libraries, and frameworks before they're introduced into production. The integration of AI into this process doesn't remove human responsibility, it multiplies its impact. When properly trained and deployed, AI can surface patterns that would otherwise go unnoticed. It can suggest changes, simulate attacks, and provide decision-makers with clarity instead of overwhelming. But to reach this point, teams must understand not only what AI is but what it is not.

AI is not a shortcut. It cannot replace sound software architecture, proper key management, or clear access control policies. What it can do, however, is extend visibility. It can watch traffic at scale, detect outliers, and learn from behavior in ways that manual systems simply can't keep up with. But only if it's integrated correctly and only if teams are prepared to respond to the insights it provides.

One of the challenges many teams face when adopting AI for fraud detection is the tendency to over-engineer. They assume complexity equals intelligence. They spend months building intricate models with limited real-world testing, only to find that the model is either too sensitive, flagging every slight variation, or not sensitive enough, letting sophisticated attacks slip through. The truth is, effective AI in financial security is often about simplicity; clear inputs, focused objectives, and constant feedback loops. It is about finding the smallest, most actionable signals that consistently lead to useful decisions.

Just as important as detection is the system's ability to respond. Identifying a threat is only part of the equation. A secure system must be able to act, by escalating, blocking, isolating, or notifying the right people at the right time. And this response must be tightly aligned with business goals. Blocking legitimate users causes revenue loss. Delaying transactions for too long leads to churn. Security that isn't aligned with product strategy will always be seen as an obstacle, rather than an enabler.

Another major pressure point is infrastructure. Financial systems today are built across cloud environments, distributed data centers, third-party services, and open banking platforms. The days of managing everything in-house are over. This means your threat surface is no longer just your code, it's also every service you depend on. One vulnerability in an upstream provider, one misconfigured permission on a third-party API, one delayed patch and the entire system becomes vulnerable.

Security engineering in this context is not just about fortifying your core. It's about managing dependencies, enforcing separation of concerns, and ensuring that your system can degrade safely if something fails. It's about designing for compromise not because you expect to lose, but because you expect to be tested. And you build so that even if one door opens, the rest of the house doesn't collapse.

This is where the mindset of modern financial software engineering must evolve. It's no longer enough to build for scale and ship quickly. You must build to protect, to adapt, and to earn trust through reliability. Users don't care how beautiful your architecture is if their money disappears. Regulators don't care how innovative your AI model is if it leads to biased decisions or unchecked access. What matters is clarity, knowing what your system is doing, why it's doing it, and how it can be trusted to do that every time.

## 1.1 The Human Layer: Where Security Is Often Breached First

No matter how robust a system is, one of its most unpredictable elements will always be the humans interacting with it. In the context of financial fraud, attackers increasingly target users and employees not through code, but through manipulation. Social engineering, phishing, credential stuffing, and insider threats remain some of the most successful methods of breaching systems. And the reason is simple: technology alone cannot account for intent.

A well-meaning employee might click a link disguised as a client invoice. A third-party contractor might be using shared credentials across systems. A user might ignore a security prompt because it slows them down. These are not flaws in code, they are flaws in human process, in training, in interface design. And they open doors that technology alone cannot fully close.

This is why secure software engineering must consider human behavior as a core design input. If a system requires five extra steps to authenticate every transaction, users will find ways around it. If developers are left out of security decisions, they will default to shortcuts. If security reviews only happen after launch, product teams will treat them as an obstacle rather than a guide.

The most secure systems in the world can still be compromised if the human layer is neglected. That means engineers must build interfaces that make secure behavior easier, not harder. It means logging activity in a way that surfaces anomalies without overwhelming the system with false positives. And it means designing processes that account for misuse—not just by attackers, but by legitimate users who are tired, distracted, or simply unaware.

Fraud doesn't always come in the form of a hack. Sometimes it arrives through a phone call, a well-written email, or an impersonated login. In all these cases, a strong technical system must be paired with clear protocols, real-time alerts, and built-in checks that are intuitive for the people using them.

## 1.2 Building Security-First Culture in Engineering Teams

Security doesn't begin and end with code. It starts with how engineering teams think, plan, and collaborate. Organizations that build secure software consistently don't just have better tools, they have better habits. They ask different questions during design reviews. They include threat modeling early in the product lifecycle. They test for edge cases, not just happy paths. And most importantly, they treat security as a shared responsibility, not as someone else's job.

In many teams, security is still treated like an external consultant, something you call in when the system is ready, or worse, when something has already gone wrong. This mindset creates tension between product and security, speed and caution, release and review. But the most mature teams break this divide. They embed security into their development culture. Engineers write code with auditability in mind. Product managers understand the cost of technical debt when it comes to risk. Security teams are invited into design conversations not just brought in to flag issues later.

This cultural shift is essential because secure software cannot be retrofitted at scale. It must be baked into the architecture, the workflows, and the team dynamics. It means having secure defaults in infrastructure-as-code templates. It means training developers to use secure authentication patterns by default. It means reviewing third-party dependencies not just for functionality, but for exposure. And it means automating what can be automated because manual reviews don't scale, and human fatigue is real.

Organizations that take security seriously also invest in clarity. They create playbooks for incident response, define ownership across environments, and maintain clear escalation paths. They treat logs not as compliance requirements, but as living tools that can tell stories in real time. And they understand that the cost of building secure systems is far less than the cost of recovering from a breach.

In the financial space, where a single misstep can ripple through regulatory bodies, customer accounts, and market sentiment, security-first culture is no longer aspirational, it's mandatory. And software engineers, whether they realize it or not, are often on the frontlines of that effort.

# CHAPTER TWO
## Principles of Secure Software Engineering for Financial Systems

Secure software engineering is not a checklist. It is a mindset, one that prioritizes clarity over shortcuts, intentionality over speed, and long-term integrity over quick wins. In the context of financial systems, this mindset becomes even more critical. The applications we build are not just pieces of code, they are infrastructures through which money flows, identities are verified, and trust is managed. And when these systems fail, the consequences are immediate and often irreversible.

The foundation of secure software engineering in finance lies in how systems are designed from the ground up. It begins before a single line of code is written with how requirements are gathered, how user journeys are mapped, and how risks are visualized. The earlier security is considered in the lifecycle, the less it costs to implement and the harder it becomes to bypass. Yet, too often, teams begin with functionality and bolt on security later, assuming it can be layered into the pipeline after the core product is stable. That assumption is the root of most security debt.

One of the first principles any engineer must internalize is the idea of "secure by design." This isn't just about avoiding bad practices. It's about designing software that inherently limits exposure. It means favoring explicit permissions over open defaults. It means building APIs that validate input rigorously, store data minimally, and fail gracefully when misuse is detected. It means making the default state of the system a safe one even when something goes wrong.

In financial systems, every component from login modules to payment gateways to audit logs, represents a potential attack surface. These systems must be architected with an awareness that attackers will try to reverse-engineer flows, exploit misconfigurations, or find inconsistencies in how sessions, tokens, and states are managed. The goal, then, is not to simply pass security tests, but to build a structure where these attack vectors are either closed or heavily monitored. And when something does slip through, the system must be able to detect, isolate, and contain the issue before it spreads.

A key part of this approach is threat modeling. Many teams treat it as a compliance requirement, running exercises to fill out templates. But at its core, threat modeling is about storytelling, mapping out how an attacker might move through a system, what data they might target, how they might try to persist, and what parts of the system are most vulnerable under pressure. It forces engineers to step outside of their intentions and consider how their work might be misused. It's not paranoia, it's realism. And it makes the resulting software stronger, more accountable, and more transparent.

Another principle often overlooked is isolation. Financial systems deal with highly sensitive data; user identities, payment credentials, transaction histories, regulatory logs. Yet many software architectures treat all services as equal, allowing broad access between components in the name of simplicity. In secure systems, access must be deliberate. Services should only be able to communicate with what they need, nothing more. User roles should be clearly defined and enforced at every layer. Secrets, keys, and credentials should be stored with strict access policies, rotated regularly, and never hardcoded into the codebase.

Logging is another area where secure engineering principles show their worth. Too often, logs are only viewed as debug tools, something useful for developers during testing. But in a financial system, logs are often the first indicator of an attack, the source of truth during a forensic investigation, and the evidence required during audits. They must be consistent, tamper-resistant, and context-rich. And they must be designed with privacy in mind. Logging sensitive data is not only a risk, it can become a violation of compliance standards. The balance, as always, lies in thoughtful design: capturing enough to understand what happened, without exposing more than what's needed.

One of the less technical, but equally vital principles in secure software engineering is simplicity. Complex systems often fail in complex ways. Every extra dependency, every clever workaround, every undocumented override creates a new layer of potential failure. In financial software where the margin for error is so small, this complexity compounds risk. Secure systems tend to be well-structured, readable, and tested. They use clear naming conventions. They avoid unnecessary abstraction. They rely on well-maintained libraries and keep their technology stacks lean. This doesn't mean innovation is sacrificed, it means innovation is delivered with clarity.

As engineering teams mature, they begin to see security as part of their development velocity, not a threat to it. Teams that embed security into their daily practices find that issues are caught earlier, feedback loops are tighter, and releases are smoother. Security reviews stop being blockers and start becoming part of the iteration cycle. Engineers learn to ask the right questions not just "does it work?" but "what could go wrong?" and "how would I break this if I had to?" These questions, asked consistently, produce code that doesn't just solve a problem but holds up under scrutiny.

Financial systems must operate under heavy regulation. This brings with it another set of constraints: audit trails, encryption standards, data residency, user consent, and more. Secure software engineering doesn't fight these constraints, it works with them. It treats them as part of the design system. When done well, compliance becomes a natural byproduct of thoughtful engineering. Not something to scramble toward, but something built into how the system works, behaves, and evolves.

What defines secure software in the financial world isn't just code. It's the thinking behind it. It's how teams collaborate, how they anticipate failure, how they approach documentation, and how they adapt over time. Secure software engineering is both a technical discipline and a cultural one. It requires tools, but also habits. Standards, but also mindset. And most importantly, it requires teams that understand that trust is not something users give freely, it is something earned with every interaction, every transaction, and every decision made behind the scenes.

One of the most difficult realities teams face when building secure financial systems is the inevitability of trade-offs. In the ideal world, every decision would lead to more security, more speed, more reliability, and more simplicity. But in real-world engineering, resources are finite, timelines are tight, and stakeholders often prioritize delivery over long-term stability. This is where secure engineering shows its true value not in the absence of compromise, but in the clarity of how compromises are made.

Trade-offs are not inherently bad. Choosing a simpler solution over a more secure one might make sense in a proof-of-concept phase, or when user adoption is uncertain. What matters is not avoiding trade-offs, but recognizing them and documenting them. Too many teams accumulate security risks unintentionally by skipping validation, delaying refactoring, or inheriting third-party code without proper evaluation. These risks don't always break systems immediately, but over time, they compound into what is often called security debt.

Security debt, like technical debt, is the accumulation of vulnerabilities, oversights, and weak design choices that haven't been addressed. Unlike performance issues or usability flaws, security debt tends to remain invisible until it becomes critical. The problem is, by the time it's visible, it's usually too late to address it without major disruption. In financial systems, this can lead to full-blown breaches, regulatory failures, or irreversible user impact.

The best way to manage security debt is to prevent it from accumulating in the first place. This requires discipline, reviewing every code change with a security lens, questioning defaults, and pushing back when deadlines pressure teams to skip essential safeguards. It means keeping dependencies up to date, setting expiration dates for temporary workarounds, and making sure every engineer understands the long-term cost of short-term decisions. It also means embedding security into definition-of-done criteria, so that incomplete or unreviewed changes don't quietly make their way into production.

Another principle that goes hand-in-hand with secure software is **auditability**. In financial environments, everything is traceable or should be. Regulators don't just want to know that a system works. They want to know how it behaves under specific scenarios, who has access to what, and how decisions are made when systems act autonomously. This is especially true when AI is involved. Systems that make real-time decisions, blocking a payment, freezing an account, escalating a threat must be able to explain what happened, why it happened, and who authorized it.

Building for auditability means writing code that leaves breadcrumbs. It means structuring logs that tie events together, capturing metadata that matters, and storing decisions in a way that can be traced back to their origin. It means avoiding "black box" logic especially in AI models where no one on the team can fully explain how an outcome was reached. Explainability isn't just a compliance requirement. It's an engineering best practice. It protects teams from blind spots and gives users and stakeholders confidence that systems are operating fairly and predictably.

One of the more nuanced aspects of secure software engineering is navigating the tension between innovation and responsibility. Financial technology is a competitive space. New features drive growth. New integrations expand markets. And teams are constantly under pressure to deliver something new, something faster, something leaner. But secure systems often require slowing down. They require testing, documentation, review, and deliberate restraint. This can create friction between product managers who want to launch and security leads who want to wait. Between developers who want to simplify and auditors who demand complexity. Between what's ideal and what's allowed.

## Why Secure Defaults Matter

One of the most powerful, yet underutilized strategies in secure software engineering is the use of secure defaults. In many systems, the default state of components, permissions, and configurations is permissive, open until explicitly restricted. This is often done in the name of usability or development flexibility, but it quietly introduces risk. When defaults are insecure, the burden shifts to developers and system administrators to identify and fix potential exposures, often without the full context or time to do so.

Secure defaults flip that script. They start with the assumption that anything not explicitly needed should be denied, disabled, or restricted. Instead of assuming access and removing it later, secure systems assume no access and grant only what is necessary. This applies to everything, from file permissions and API routes to user roles and system integrations. It might slow things down at first, but over time, it significantly reduces the number of entry points that need to be monitored, tested, and defended.

In a financial system, where sensitive data flows through multiple layers, secure defaults serve as a safety net. If something is misconfigured or partially deployed, the system errs on the side of caution not exposure. And when engineers adopt this mindset consistently, they begin to design features that only activate when conditions are met, rather than assuming that every user or service will always follow the intended flow. This principle, sometimes summarized as "fail safe, not fail open" is one of the most valuable habits a security-minded engineer can develop.

# Role of Documentation in Security

Documentation is often viewed as an afterthought in software projects, something to be polished for clients or auditors after the system is deployed. But in secure engineering, documentation is infrastructure. It guides how teams handle edge cases, how incidents are escalated, and how knowledge is transferred when team members rotate. In fast-paced development environments, security measures that aren't documented might as well not exist.

Well-documented systems allow security teams to audit configurations without guessing. They help new engineers understand what's been implemented and why. They give operations teams the context to investigate anomalies quickly, and they give compliance teams the materials they need to meet regulatory standards. Most importantly, documentation serves as a checkpoint against assumptions. It forces teams to articulate decisions, revisit trade-offs, and consider whether the system is still aligned with its security goals.

In financial platforms, where features evolve and regulations shift, documentation becomes the historical record of risk decisions. Why was a control implemented? Why was a threshold set? Why does a model exclude certain data? These answers don't just live in code, they must live in conversation, and good documentation captures that conversation in a way that future teams can trust.

Moreover, with AI now playing an increasing role in financial decision-making, documentation also becomes essential for explainability. If an AI-powered fraud detection model blocks a user's transaction, teams must be able to explain what inputs led to that decision, how the model behaved under those inputs, and what options exist for remediation. Without this trail, trust breaks down, internally and externally.

## Engineering Trust at Scale

Trust is the silent foundation of every financial system. Users trust that their money is safe. Partners trust that their integrations won't expose them. Regulators trust that platforms are operating within acceptable bounds. And teams trust that the systems they build will behave predictably under stress. But trust doesn't scale automatically, it must be engineered.

To build trust into software systems, especially at scale, teams must prioritize transparency and predictability. Features should behave consistently, not just under normal conditions, but under failure. Logs should tell a coherent story, not a fragmented series of clues. Risk flags and alerts should be meaningful not just noise that teams learn to ignore. And user-facing messages must be clear, so people know when something has gone wrong and what to do about it.

Scalable trust also means building systems that don't rely on heroic individuals. A secure platform shouldn't fall apart when one engineer leaves or one team member forgets a manual step. Trust is built through redundancy, automation, repeatability, and culture.

It's reinforced through security drills, system reviews, and incident retrospectives that focus not on blame, but on learning.

At the heart of all this is the understanding that trust isn't given, it's earned. And in financial software, it's earned every time a transaction goes through cleanly, every time a threat is blocked silently, every time a system recovers from an unexpected state without data loss or panic. Secure engineering, then, becomes an act of stewardship. Not just of systems, but of people's confidence in those systems. And that, more than any tool or framework, is what makes a platform truly secure.

# CHAPTER THREE
## AI in Cybersecurity: Fundamentals and Use Cases

Artificial intelligence has moved far beyond the realm of theoretical excitement. In financial cybersecurity, it now plays a central role in how threats are detected, how responses are triggered, and how systems adapt to evolving behavior. The growing complexity of digital infrastructure, combined with the volume, speed, and variability of financial transactions has made traditional rule-based systems insufficient for long-term protection. AI doesn't replace these systems. Rather, it augments them, filling in the gaps where static logic fails to keep up.

Understanding AI's place in cybersecurity begins with a recognition of its core strength: pattern recognition at scale. Where human analysts or rule engines may overlook weak signals, AI models especially those trained on time-series data or behavioral baselines can identify subtle, often non-obvious indicators of potential fraud or compromise. These indicators may show up as unusual login times, irregular transaction paths, inconsistent device fingerprints, or repeated access from dynamically shifting IP blocks. On their own, each of these signals might not trigger a flag. But when viewed through a learning system that understands the context of user behavior, they form a narrative that suggests something is off.

In financial systems, this is especially important because fraud rarely presents itself in isolation. It hides in the margins. It mimics normal activity. It adapts to the thresholds and static rules it knows systems rely on. That's why AI is most powerful when deployed in environments where historical data can be used to define not just what's acceptable, but what's probable. Probability is key, because good fraud detection doesn't catch everything, but it should catch what matters with a high degree of confidence, and without overwhelming human teams with noise.

Machine learning models used in cybersecurity vary in approach. Some are supervised, trained on labeled datasets where past incidents are used to teach the model what to look for. Others are unsupervised, allowing the model to determine for itself what counts as "normal" by analyzing raw behavior across time. Semi-supervised models and reinforcement learning approaches are emerging as well, giving systems the ability to adjust their responses based on success or feedback loops. What matters is not just the model architecture, but the way it's applied in the system.

One common use case in financial cybersecurity is anomaly detection. Here, AI models are trained to learn a baseline of user behavior how often a user logs in, from which locations, using which devices, and what kind of transactions they typically perform. When that behavior deviates in significant or suspicious ways, the model raises a flag. In an ideal system, this doesn't lead to immediate blocks or lockouts, but rather initiates a tiered response, maybe asking for additional verification, throttling transaction speed, or sending a real-time alert to a monitoring team. AI here acts as a filter, narrowing down millions of benign activities to the few that deserve closer inspection.

Another important use case is in phishing and malware detection. AI-powered email filters and endpoint protection tools can now analyze not just the content of messages or files, but their structure, origin, intent, and behavior over time. These systems often use natural language processing (NLP) to detect manipulative language or sentiment, and behavioral analysis to monitor whether users interact with the message in dangerous ways, like clicking suspicious links or entering credentials into spoofed sites. In financial organizations, where executives are high-value targets and internal tools are often email-accessible, this kind of defense is critical.

In real-time transaction monitoring, AI systems go even deeper. Instead of merely scanning for blacklisted accounts or regions, they analyze how money moves. They detect velocity, how fast funds are being transferred, in what increments, and whether similar patterns have preceded fraud elsewhere. These models can pick up when fraud is being spread out to avoid detection thresholds or when a user's behavior shifts just slightly over time, slow enough to avoid human suspicion, but fast enough to be meaningful. This is the kind of nuance AI is uniquely suited to handle.

But deploying AI in cybersecurity isn't without its challenges. One major risk is overfitting, where the model learns the training data too well and fails to generalize to new or evolving threats. Another is bias, if training data skews toward specific user types, behaviors, or locations, the model may make inaccurate or unfair decisions in production. This is particularly sensitive in financial systems, where decisions like freezing an account or rejecting a transaction carry real-world consequences. That's why explainability is becoming a major focus in AI-powered security. Stakeholders, whether internal auditors, compliance officers, or even customers must be able to understand why the system took the action it did.

It's also essential to understand that AI, while powerful, is not self-maintaining. Models degrade over time. Threat actors adapt. User behavior changes. What was "normal" a month ago may no longer be accurate. This means AI models in cybersecurity require regular retraining, periodic evaluation, and governance controls that ensure updates are safe, intentional, and well-documented. Without this, AI can become a liability, acting on outdated assumptions, reinforcing flawed decisions, or even being manipulated by adversaries who've studied the model's behavior.

Security teams must also think about how AI integrates into their broader system. AI is not a separate tool to be plugged in. It must be embedded into the workflows of engineering, DevOps, monitoring, and incident response. A fraud alert that sits in a dashboard but never reaches the right team in time is just as useless as one that was never raised. AI can improve detection, but its value is only realized when the organization is structured to act on it.

One of the most underestimated challenges in AI adoption is not in the technology itself, but in the human systems that surround it. While it's true that AI can detect and respond to threats faster than traditional tools, its effectiveness is heavily dependent on how well organizations structure their operations to support it. Teams must be trained to interpret model output, distinguish between true and false positives, and feed meaningful feedback into the system to improve future performance. Without this collaboration, even the most sophisticated models risk becoming static tools, powerful but directionless.

In fast-paced financial environments, where teams are managing uptime, new features, regulatory changes, and user support all at once, AI systems must be built with the understanding that false alarms have a cost. If a model produces too many false positives, trust erodes. Security analysts begin to overlook critical alerts, teams become desensitized to system flags, and over time, legitimate threats may slip through unnoticed. On the other hand, under-sensitive models that fail to flag real anomalies pose an even greater risk, allowing attackers to exploit blind spots without resistance.

This delicate balance underscores why AI in cybersecurity should not be seen as a black box solution, but as a strategic component in a larger, well-governed architecture. The best implementations make model behavior transparent. They log decision paths, expose confidence scores, and allow for human intervention where uncertainty exists. More mature systems even allow for adjustable thresholds that can be tuned based on changing risk appetite or operational load—tightening controls during periods of known threat activity and relaxing them when teams are under heavy strain.

Another emerging use case involves AI-assisted identity verification and behavioral biometrics. These tools are becoming increasingly important in financial applications, especially in regions where identity documents may be limited or inconsistent. AI models can now evaluate typing speed, touchscreen gestures, navigation patterns, and even the angle at which a phone is held to determine whether the person using an account is behaving like its usual owner. When paired with traditional authentication methods, these invisible behavioral checks add an additional layer of frictionless security, making it much harder for stolen credentials alone to be useful.

We're also seeing AI used in synthetic fraud detection, an area that's rapidly growing in complexity. Synthetic fraud involves creating fake identities that appear real enough to pass traditional checks, often built using fragments of legitimate data (like stolen SSNs or birthdates) combined with fabricated profiles. AI is helping to counter this by mapping the relationships between users, devices, IP addresses, and transaction behavior identifying clusters that appear statistically unlikely or exhibit signs of artificial construction. These insights are difficult to produce manually but are well-suited to unsupervised learning techniques and graph-based models.

Yet, in all these examples, it's important to remember that AI is only as good as the data it sees. Bias in training data leads to biased outcomes. Gaps in data lead to blind spots in detection. And poor labeling practices can reinforce incorrect patterns that grow stronger over time. That's why data engineering is a critical part of AI-powered cybersecurity. It's not just about collecting logs or storing transactions, it's about curating, cleaning, labeling, and securing the data so that it can support real intelligence, not artificial assumptions.

In financial environments, this challenge is amplified by the need for privacy and compliance. Data cannot be freely copied, exported, or mixed. There are legal limits on what can be processed, where it can be stored, and how long it can be retained. This makes the design of AI systems far more complex than in other industries. Models must be efficient enough to work with what data is legally accessible. Anonymization must be applied in ways that retain signal while protecting identity. And every decision made by the system must be logged in a way that is explainable not just for auditors, but for customers who may question why their transaction was blocked or delayed.

It's also worth addressing the psychological dimension of AI-driven systems. As organizations introduce more intelligent tools into their cybersecurity infrastructure, a subtle risk emerges: the temptation to defer too much responsibility to the machine. When a system performs well, there's a tendency to stop questioning it, to stop challenging its decisions, and to assume its outputs are always correct. This overreliance creates a dangerous form of complacency. It can mask new attack patterns that fall outside the model's learned behavior. It can cause organizations to ignore edge cases. And in the worst scenarios, it can result in systems making harmful decisions without oversight.

The best use of AI in cybersecurity is not as a replacement for human judgment, but as a multiplier of it. AI should extend what humans can observe, accelerate how fast they can respond, and provide guidance that is rooted in probabilistic insight rather than gut feeling. But it should always allow for review. It should invite challenge. And it should be continuously tested against real-world scenarios to ensure it's still aligned with the threats it was built to defend against.

## The Cost of Misclassification in AI-Powered Security

Every decision made by an AI system in a cybersecurity context carries weight. In many industries, a misclassification may simply cause inconvenience. But in financial systems, where trust and money intersect, the stakes are higher. A single decision, wrongly denying a transaction, freezing an account, or allowing a fraudulent payment to proceed can trigger a chain reaction of consequences. Misclassification, in this context, is not just a data issue. It's a business risk, a customer experience crisis, and in some cases, a regulatory liability.

False positives and false negatives are not abstract concerns. They are real moments that affect real people. When a legitimate user is blocked from accessing their account because an AI model incorrectly classified their behavior as suspicious, the damage isn't just transactional, it's emotional. Frustration builds. Confidence drops. That user may start to doubt whether the platform is reliable. Worse, they may leave. In high-churn markets like digital banking or payment apps, every false positive becomes an opportunity for the competition to step in.

On the other hand, false negatives where fraud goes undetected are perhaps even more damaging. A successful fraud attack doesn't just impact one transaction. It opens the door to escalation. Fraudsters test systems slowly, using stolen credentials or synthetic identities to explore what the system lets them do. Once they've mapped the boundaries, they act decisively. If an AI system misses these signals, the breach doesn't just grow in size, it gains momentum. And once users discover their data or funds were compromised, the trust lost can be irreversible.

This is why tuning an AI system is both art and science. It requires constant iteration, grounded in data but guided by human judgment. It also demands more than just technical tuning, it requires collaboration across teams. Product managers must understand how model decisions affect user flows. Compliance officers must weigh in on what regulatory boundaries must be respected. Engineers must translate business goals into risk thresholds. And data scientists must continuously evaluate performance metrics like precision, recall, and AUC but also qualitative signals from the front lines: support tickets, user complaints, and analyst feedback.

Calibration is not a one-time exercise. It must happen continuously. Models must be re-evaluated against evolving patterns of use, new forms of fraud, and shifts in business logic. For example, a feature that increases transaction volume like enabling batch transfers or peer-to-peer splitting can dramatically change what "normal behavior" looks like. If the model isn't updated to understand this change, it may misclassify a legitimate spike in usage as fraudulent activity. Inversely, a fraud ring might start adapting to the model's blind spots, slowing down transactions, mimicking average user behavior, or operating during off-hours. These edge cases often emerge only through human-in-the-loop review and feedback loops that are built into the AI deployment lifecycle.

Financial institutions also have to navigate the regulatory implications of misclassification. In regions with strong data protection and consumer rights laws, blocking a user's account or rejecting a transaction without clear justification can trigger compliance audits. If the decision was made by an opaque algorithm with no audit trail, the organization is left exposed, not just to fines, but to legal challenges. Regulators are increasingly asking for explainability in AI decisions. That means every classification should be traceable, reproducible, and defensible. Not just to internal stakeholders but to external reviewers, partners, and sometimes, the users themselves.

The reality is that no AI model will ever be perfect. But the goal is not perfection, it is proportionate, consistent, and explainable decision-making. The cost of misclassification can never be eliminated, but it can be managed, minimized, and understood. And for that, organizations need more than models. They need processes, policies, and people trained to act on the outcomes responsibly.

## Moving from Detection to Intelligence

Many organizations stop at detection when deploying AI in cybersecurity. They build or buy systems that can flag anomalies, score transactions, and alert teams when something seems off. And while detection is critical, it is only the beginning. True security maturity comes from moving beyond alerts to systems that generate insight, support analysis, and drive intelligent action. This evolution, from detection to intelligence is the key to staying ahead in a threat landscape that's constantly shifting.

Intelligence, in this context, is not just about identifying when something is wrong. It's about understanding why, how often, under what conditions, and what can be done about it. It's about identifying the actor behind the behavior, recognizing the tools they're using, predicting their next move, and correlating activity across time, systems, and users. In short, it's about turning raw detection signals into narratives of intent and doing so fast enough to prevent harm.

Consider an organization with a fraud detection model that flags repeated logins from new devices. On its own, this alert may be helpful. But if paired with device fingerprinting, network mapping, geo-velocity analysis, and behavioral biometrics, the same system can now piece together whether this is a genuine user switching devices or a fraudster testing access with leaked credentials. And if similar patterns are seen across multiple accounts, the system may escalate the event from a single anomaly to a coordinated campaign, triggering higher-level responses.

This is the power of intelligence: the ability to connect dots at scale, and to do so continuously. It relies not just on model performance, but on data infrastructure, tagging standards, and feedback integration. Analysts and engineers must work together to label incident data accurately, ensuring that future training cycles learn from the past not just technically, but contextually. Threat intelligence feeds can be integrated to enrich internal data, providing signals about known fraud actors, compromised data sources, or evolving attack vectors.

As systems become more intelligent, they can start offering recommendations, not just alerts. For example, suggesting which accounts should undergo a secondary verification process, which transactions should be delayed for human review, or which behavioral patterns suggest insider risk. These insights empower teams to act with confidence and clarity. They shift security from being a reactive function to a strategic asset, one that helps guide product decisions, influence risk policies, and even shape customer onboarding flows.

But intelligence at this level doesn't come automatically. It requires deliberate architecture. Data pipelines must be clean, modular, and secure. AI models must be versioned, monitored, and continuously validated. Analysts must have interfaces that allow them to drill into decisions and provide structured feedback. And executives must invest not only in tools, but in the organizational literacy required to interpret and act on what those tools reveal.

When this foundation is in place, AI becomes more than a filter, it becomes an ally. It amplifies visibility. It accelerates response. And it gives organizations the ability to evolve faster than the threats they face. In a world where cyberattacks are increasingly automated, scalable, and sophisticated, intelligence is no longer a luxury, it is the currency of resilience.

Gbenga Akingbulere

# CHAPTER FOUR
## Designing AI-Powered Fraud Detection Systems

Every financial platform, no matter how small or large, carries the weight of one unrelenting question: can we trust this system with our money? Behind that question is another, more operational one: can this system detect and stop fraud without breaking the user experience? The challenge is delicate. Fraud detection must be both invisible and immediate, constantly running in the background, learning from behavior, adapting to new patterns, and intervening only when truly necessary. The ability to design such a system; where accuracy, speed, and scale align is one of the most defining responsibilities of today's software engineers and AI practitioners.

At the center of an AI-powered fraud detection system lies a model or, more commonly, a group of models trained to differentiate between legitimate and suspicious activity. But before any model is selected, teams must define what fraud looks like in their context.

Fraud is not a fixed concept. In a peer-to-peer payment app, it might be rapid-fire transfers to a newly added recipient. In a mobile lending platform, it might be coordinated identity creation from a shared device. In a cross-border banking system, it might be microtransactions structured to evade compliance checks. Each platform has its own fingerprint of risk, shaped by its architecture, users, markets, and product flows.

Designing for this reality means going beyond academic definitions. It means working with data teams, product leads, and fraud analysts to map the types of abuse that have occurred in the past and the ones that haven't occurred yet but could. This kind of forward-looking threat modeling is critical. It allows systems to be designed not only to catch fraud that has already happened, but to **predict and prevent** fraud that is yet to emerge. That's where AI excels not in catching what we already know, but in surfacing what we can't yet see.

Once fraud patterns are defined, data becomes the next cornerstone. The quality of a model is never better than the quality of its training data. This data must be clean, labeled, representative, and broad enough to capture a range of behaviors. It must also be processed ethically, respecting user privacy, regulatory limits, and consent boundaries. Financial data is often fragmented across systems, some in logs, some in databases, some in partner platforms. Building a cohesive fraud detection system means pulling together this data in a way that preserves context while minimizing exposure.

The features derived from this data, the inputs that a model uses to learn are where domain knowledge and engineering rigor meet. It's not enough to feed the model transaction amounts or timestamps. Features need to reflect behavior. For example, time since last login, velocity of recent transactions, similarity to previous patterns, distance between user IP and registered location, or the variance in device identifiers across a 24-hour window. These derived insights are often more powerful than raw values. They enable the model to learn not just what happened, but what that behavior might mean in context.

With features prepared, the question of model selection arises. In many real-world deployments, simpler models outperform complex ones not because they are smarter, but because they are faster to interpret, easier to tune, and more resilient to data inconsistencies. Logistic regression, decision trees, and random forests often perform well in early stages. As systems mature, organizations may evolve toward ensemble methods or neural networks that can handle larger-scale data and deeper pattern recognition. The goal is always the same: reliable, explainable, and adaptable detection.

Yet no model, no matter how well tuned, is immune to drift. User behavior changes. Fraud evolves. Business logic shifts. What worked yesterday may underperform tomorrow. This is why retraining infrastructure is just as important as the model itself. Systems must be able to evaluate performance continuously, gather new labels from analyst feedback, and roll out new model versions safely. CI/CD for machine learning commonly called MLOps is essential in fraud detection. Without it, models stagnate, and risk silently grows.

Deployment is another layer of complexity. Fraud detection systems must operate in real time or near real time. Delays in decision-making can lead to financial losses, user dissatisfaction, or compliance breaches. This means models must be optimized not just for accuracy, but for latency. Engineering teams must decide where inference happens, at the edge, in an API layer, or in a real-time streaming engine. They must also build in fallbacks: if the model is unavailable, what decision should the system make? If a prediction is inconclusive, should the transaction be delayed, reviewed, or allowed?

Beyond deployment lies integration. Fraud detection models must plug seamlessly into existing infrastructure, account systems, transaction engines, alerting platforms, and escalation workflows. The decision a model makes cannot live in isolation. It must trigger action. That action must be traceable. And the entire chain, from event to decision to response must be logged in a way that supports compliance, analysis, and auditability. This is where model monitoring, feedback loops, and decision logging come into play.

Equally important is the human interface. Fraud detection is not a fully automated process. There will always be edge cases. Some decisions require investigation, escalation, or human override. The systems that work best are those that balance autonomy with control. They flag risk, but they don't act blindly. They provide scores, reasons, and historical context so that human analysts can act with clarity. And they allow for post-decision feedback, was the alert useful? Was the fraud real? Should this behavior be reclassified in future training?

Trust is also a factor. Users must believe that the system protects without intruding. They must understand why an action was taken, especially if their transaction was blocked or their account flagged. This is why explainability is not just for internal teams, it is part of user experience design. Messages must be clear, recovery steps must be easy, and processes must not punish users for the system's caution.

What distinguishes a truly robust fraud detection system isn't just how well it performs under known conditions, but how gracefully it handles the unknown. Fraud evolves. Attackers shift strategies. A new payment feature, an expanded user base, or even a promotional campaign can suddenly change the nature of system traffic. In this environment, adaptability is not just a bonus, it's a core requirement.

Adaptability begins with how a system responds to its own blind spots. There will always be moments when a fraudulent transaction slips through undetected, or when a model is unsure how to classify an activity. These moments aren't failures, they are feedback. But for that feedback to be valuable, the system must be designed to capture it. This means building event traceability into every decision, logging confidence scores, collecting analyst notes, and structuring data in a way that makes retraining efficient. A system that learns only from success is limited. The best systems learn from ambiguity, exceptions, and even mistakes.

A common mistake in early fraud detection deployments is assuming that detection is a solved problem that once a model is deployed, the threat has been handled. But many teams have learned the hard way that initial success can lead to complacency. Models that perform well at launch may degrade quietly. They may begin to underperform as fraudsters adapt to their logic. In some cases, internal shifts in business processes, like changes in account recovery workflows or promotional campaign eligibility; introduce new fraud vectors that were never accounted for in the original design. Without continuous validation, these blind spots remain undetected until they're exploited at scale.

History is filled with real-world lessons. Systems that focused solely on transactional anomalies missed coordinated social engineering attacks. Platforms that treated all users the same failed to identify synthetic identity fraud hiding behind seemingly normal behavior. Some organizations failed to isolate fraud risk between different product verticals, allowing a bad actor flagged in one part of the system to operate freely in another. These failures didn't stem from bad intentions or lack of talent. They stemmed from systems built without contextual intelligence, without holistic visibility, and without mechanisms for course correction.

This is why interdisciplinary collaboration is essential. Fraud detection doesn't belong solely to data scientists or backend engineers. It requires the insights of compliance officers who understand legal thresholds, product managers who grasp user behavior patterns, operations staff who handle customer escalations, and even marketing teams who anticipate how users might exploit or misunderstand new features. When fraud detection is siloed, it becomes brittle. When it's cross-functional, it becomes strategic.

Cross-team collaboration also ensures that models aren't developed in isolation from the systems they serve. A machine learning engineer may see a spike in transaction volume as "noise," while a product manager understands it as the result of a new feature rollout. A support analyst might interpret multiple failed login attempts as suspicious, while a designer knows it's linked to a recent UX change in password recovery. These perspectives, shared early and often, prevent costly misinterpretations and help models remain grounded in reality.

This culture of cross-functional feedback must be supported by tooling, process, and leadership. Systems should allow non-technical users to review flagged transactions, submit notes, and participate in decision calibration. Analysts should be trained not only to respond to alerts, but to help refine the models generating them. Engineers should be encouraged to write code that supports experimentation and observation not just performance. And leadership must create space for iteration, accepting that fraud detection is an evolving discipline, not a fixed feature.

Beyond the technical and collaborative aspects, there is a broader organizational mindset that must be cultivated: resilience over perfection. No fraud detection system will catch everything. And those that attempt to will likely create unnecessary friction for legitimate users. The goal is not to eliminate all risk, but to manage it intelligently. This means knowing when to act, when to escalate, and when to monitor. It means recognizing that overreaction can be just as damaging as underreaction, particularly in environments where financial trust is fragile.

Resilience also means building for failure. Not just for model failure, but for systemic failure: if a fraud detection service goes down, can the system degrade safely? If an alert pipeline is delayed, can teams still trace critical activity? If a decision is contested by a user, is there a clear and fair path for review? These are questions that are rarely asked during initial development, but they are the questions that determine how well a system performs when it's truly tested.

## Designing for Transparency in AI Decision-Making

As AI systems take on a larger role in determining the outcomes of high-stakes financial decisions, the demand for transparency becomes non-negotiable. Financial fraud detection doesn't just sit in the background—it touches users directly. It decides whether a payment goes through, whether an account is suspended, or whether access to digital banking tools is delayed. These are deeply personal moments for users, and they expect answers. "Why was I blocked?" "Why is this suspicious?" "What happens next?" A system that can't explain itself will struggle to earn or keep trust.

Internally, this lack of clarity becomes a technical liability. When analysts can't interpret why a model made a decision, their job becomes guesswork. Escalations take longer to resolve, root cause analysis becomes muddled, and feedback loops break down. This not only increases operational burden but weakens the very performance of the system over time. The most sophisticated models in the world are of little value if no one not even the teams maintaining them, can tell how they think.

Explainable AI (XAI) practices aim to address this. These include tools and frameworks that expose the internal logic of models, such as SHAP values, LIME explanations, and interpretable machine learning libraries that allow teams to highlight which features were most influential in each decision. These tools are especially important when models are deployed across global regions where legal requirements demand a higher level of accountability. In jurisdictions governed by GDPR, for instance, users have the right to an explanation when an automated system impacts them. Transparent systems help institutions stay on the right side of these regulations.

But transparency doesn't end with technical introspection. It extends to how information is communicated to users and stakeholders. Effective fraud systems incorporate UI/UX design principles that help users understand what went wrong without overwhelming them. They offer guided recovery steps, opportunities for contesting decisions, and real-time notifications that keep users in the loop. Internally, dashboards must provide clear, structured views of model performance, broken down by time, region, type of threat, and accuracy rate. This allows stakeholders, from engineering to compliance to make decisions from a place of insight, not assumption.

Transparent systems also create institutional memory. They capture not just what was decided, but why, under what conditions, and with what supporting evidence. This makes audits easier, model retraining more efficient, and strategic discussions around risk more grounded. When systems can tell their own story clearly, they become reliable, not just as technical tools, but as strategic assets.

## Combating Adaptive Fraud with Adaptive Models

The most persistent myth in AI fraud detection is that once a model is trained and deployed, the job is done. The truth is the exact opposite. Deploying a model is the beginning; not the end of the lifecycle. Fraudsters study how fraud models behave. They experiment, test limits, and continuously adjust tactics to outsmart detection. They operate with agility, creativity, and little regard for system boundaries. If models don't evolve just as rapidly, they become obsolete.

Adaptive fraud is particularly dangerous because it disguises itself within the boundaries of what the system already sees as normal. Attackers learn how thresholds are set. They test velocity limits.

They monitor what behavior gets flagged and what slides through. Some even use AI themselves to simulate real-user behavior patterns and manipulate machine learning inputs.

To keep pace, detection systems must adopt **continuous learning**. This includes mechanisms for automated retraining, feature refresh, and anomaly response injection. It also includes intelligent drift detection, monitoring the input data and alerting engineers when key variables begin to shift. This shift might not signal fraud directly, it could indicate new types of users, expanded product use, or subtle changes in how existing customers interact with the system. Adaptive models don't panic in the face of change, they adjust.

Advanced techniques like online learning, transfer learning, and reinforcement learning can offer even deeper adaptability. Online learning allows models to update their parameters incrementally as new data flows in. Transfer learning enables systems to inherit knowledge from one environment and apply it in another; useful when expanding to new markets with limited labeled data. Reinforcement learning gives models the ability to learn from trial and error, adjusting their behavior based on long-term reward outcomes, such as minimizing false positives over a moving window.

But adaptability must be governed. A model that adjusts too quickly, without constraints, risks overfitting to noise or bias. That's why guardrails must be placed around adaptive behavior. Human-in-the-loop verification, staged rollouts, validation against holdout sets, and rollback strategies are essential. Adaptation without structure creates chaos. Structured adaptation creates resilience.

## Measuring Success Beyond Accuracy

Ask most teams deploying fraud detection systems how they're doing, and the answer often starts with accuracy: "Our model is 98% accurate." But what does that really mean? Accuracy as a standalone metric is deceptive. In highly imbalanced datasets where 99% of users are legitimate, predicting "not fraud" for every transaction would still deliver high accuracy. But it would be a catastrophic failure.

Real performance must be evaluated through a combination of precision, recall, specificity, sensitivity, AUC scores, and operational metrics. But even these numbers, when presented in isolation, miss the point. What matters most is the downstream impact of the model's behavior. How is the model affecting fraud rates? How is it impacting customer satisfaction? Are transaction abandonment rates increasing due to friction? Is analyst workload going down because alerts are cleaner? Is there a measurable improvement in regulatory standing or audit outcomes?

Measuring success also means understanding business alignment. A model that blocks high-risk transactions may be effective in preventing loss, but if it also reduces high-value customer onboarding, it might be doing more harm than good. Models must be evaluated not just on technical effectiveness, but on strategic fit.

Are they enabling growth? Are they providing insights to other departments like marketing, customer support, or legal? Are they shaping better policy decisions based on real data?

Organizations mature when they begin to see success as multidimensional. They balance fraud prevention with customer experience, operational efficiency with system resilience, and data science performance with ethical design. Teams that embrace this broader definition of success make better decisions, improve faster, and stay relevant longer.

## Building Long-Term Strategic Advantage Through Security

Too many organizations still treat security as an expense, something necessary but burdensome. In reality, security done right is one of the most powerful levers for competitive differentiation. When customers believe their funds and identities are safe, they use platforms more frequently, store more value, and refer more people. When partners see mature fraud systems in place, they are more likely to collaborate, invest, or integrate. When regulators see proactive transparency and compliance infrastructure, they build more trust. Security creates gravity.

Strategically, fraud detection systems also unlock innovation. They allow product teams to test new features, open riskier channels, and experiment with business models because the detection safety net is in place. A strong fraud system means a product doesn't have to move slowly just to stay safe. It can move smartly.

Moreover, in industries where reputation is everything, avoiding one high-profile breach can preserve years of brand equity. In financial services, trust is hard-won and easily lost. Having systems that quietly stop fraud behind the scenes isn't just protective, it's profitable.

The most forward-thinking companies treat AI-powered fraud systems as more than infrastructure, they treat them as platforms. Platforms that support experimentation, collaboration, customer empathy, and market confidence. These systems aren't just defensive, they're offensive assets in the race for market share, regulatory partnership, and user loyalty.

# CHAPTER FIVE

## Scaling Secure Systems: Cloud-Native Architecture for AI-Driven Fraud Detection

Building a fraud detection system that works at small scale is a milestone. But making it work at scale, under unpredictable demand, cross-border transactions, third-party integrations, and real-time user flows is an entirely different kind of challenge. Scaling is not just a matter of expanding compute or memory. In security, scaling means resilience. It means speed under stress. It means detecting, processing, and acting on threats without latency, bottlenecks, or loss of visibility. This is where cloud-native architecture becomes not just useful, but necessary.

The promise of cloud-native infrastructure is its flexibility. Resources scale automatically, services are loosely coupled, deployment is continuous and monitoring is pervasive. These are not just features, they are strategic capabilities for a system that must remain available, intelligent, and defensible at every layer. In a financial environment where fraud happens in milliseconds, the infrastructure must respond just as quickly. A lag of three seconds can mean the difference between an intercepted transaction and a completed theft.

To build fraud systems that scale, the first architectural principle is modularity. Every component, feature extraction, model inference, alert handling, data storage should be designed as an independent service, communicating over secure APIs, with clear contracts and retry mechanisms. This not only enables scaling individual parts of the pipeline based on demand (for example, increasing model instances during peak hours) but also isolates failures. If the inference engine slows down, the feature service shouldn't crash. If the alerting queue backs up, transactions can still be processed with degraded response or fallbacks.

In the cloud-native world, statelessness is an ally. Stateless services are easier to scale horizontally. They can be restarted without coordination, deployed globally, and load-balanced across regions. This is crucial for fraud systems that must monitor users in different time zones, across different products, and on different networks. Statelessness, however, doesn't mean disconnected. The system must still maintain context, user sessions, transaction history, device profiles but it does so through distributed caching, centralized state stores, and message-based coordination instead of tight coupling.

Latency is another key consideration. AI-powered fraud detection must happen in near real-time. If a system takes too long to analyze a transaction, the user experience suffers or worse, the fraud succeeds. Achieving low-latency inference requires optimizations at every level. Models must be compressed or compiled for fast execution. Serving infrastructure must be geographically distributed, bringing decision-making closer to the user. Caches must be warm, endpoints must be resilient, and failovers must be automatic.

But speed means nothing without observability. In a cloud-native fraud platform, visibility is everything. Engineers must be able to trace decisions end-to-end, from raw transaction to risk score to action taken. Logs must be structured, rich, and queryable. Metrics must reflect business impact; alert rate, false positive ratio, fraud blocked, system uptime not just technical throughput. And tracing must illuminate dependencies between services, so that performance degradation in one component doesn't remain invisible.

Infrastructure-as-code plays a major role here. With declarative tools like Terraform or Pulumi, environments can be recreated, tested, and audited with confidence. Security groups, firewalls, encryption policies, and service identities can be codified, versioned, and reviewed like application code. This allows teams to ship infrastructure changes with the same discipline they apply to features. It also reduces the chances of misconfigurations; one of the most common causes of security breaches in cloud systems.

Another core element of scalable fraud architecture is data streaming. Batch systems, while useful for reporting and model training, are often too slow for real-time fraud defense. Systems must ingest and process data as it arrives, transaction metadata, session behavior, device telemetry, login attempts. Streaming platforms like Kafka, Pulsar, or Kinesis allow fraud pipelines to consume, enrich, and route data with sub-second latency. This enables real-time scoring, dynamic rule evaluation, and event-driven response orchestration. Fraud detection becomes not a daily report, but a continuous reflex.

High-scale fraud detection also demands secure data lakes and feature stores. These storage layers allow models to train on massive amounts of historical data without compromising performance or compliance. They separate raw from curated data, enable fine-grained access control, and support data versioning for repeatable experiments. This is especially important in financial systems where data provenance, consent, and auditability are legal requirements, not just technical conveniences.

One challenge often faced when scaling is managing multi-tenant data environments. In platforms that serve multiple clients or user segments, isolation becomes essential. Each tenant must be protected from cross-data contamination, both for privacy and security. Detection models must be tenant-aware, understanding the specific risk profiles and behavioral norms of each cohort. Infrastructure must enforce separation at the storage, compute, and access level. Even when detection logic is shared, execution contexts should be scoped tightly to prevent data leaks or logic flaws.

Security in a scalable system is also about zero-trust architecture. In large cloud-native deployments, assuming anything is safe by default is a risk. Every service must authenticate, authorize, and encrypt. Least privilege access is the rule. Secrets are stored in vaults, rotated frequently, and audited continuously. Internal APIs are locked down. Monitoring isn't just external, it's internal, with service-to-service traffic inspected and anomalous patterns flagged, even if the calls never leave the infrastructure boundary.

Scaling a fraud detection system in the cloud means preparing for the unexpected. Infrastructure must not only scale up, it must fail gracefully. Canary deployments, blue-green rollouts, chaos testing, auto-scaling triggers, and load-shedding policies are all part of the design. Because at the moment when fraud attempts spike; when a phishing campaign spreads, when bots begin probing the login endpoints, when credential stuffing begins, the system must not slow down. It must rise to the occasion, absorb the pressure, and protect the platform without sacrificing performance or experience.

As systems scale, they don't just inherit technical complexity, they inherit regulatory responsibility. In financial systems, this responsibility is heavy. Every endpoint, every integration, every backup policy must respect data laws, customer rights, and financial system integrity. The beauty of cloud-native systems, their elasticity, speed, and distributed power can become a risk if not tempered with regulatory foresight. You're not just building infrastructure that works; you're building infrastructure that's legally defensible, regionally compliant, and globally trusted.

Compliance in the cloud is a layered challenge. You're not only subject to internal security standards or partner expectations, but also to international regulations like GDPR, PCI DSS, PSD2, CCPA, and local financial compliance rules, each of which defines its own expectations for encryption, data residency, access logging, and breach response. In a multi-cloud or hybrid deployment, where data moves across environments or sits in geographically diverse zones, compliance isn't just about ticking checkboxes. It requires architectural intention.

One core principle of design is data residency awareness, understanding exactly where data lives, where it's processed, and where it's backed up. Many countries require that certain types of financial data remain within national borders or be encrypted under local keys. In practice, this means detection pipelines must be regionally aware. A model running in Europe may need to use only European data. A log aggregation tool operating globally must be able to mask, redact, or separate user records depending on jurisdiction. Centralization may be efficient, but it often conflicts with residency rules. Engineers must find the balance between performance and sovereignty, between real-time risk scoring and lawful data separation.

This is where geo-partitioned design becomes essential. Cloud-native fraud systems should be built to replicate core detection logic across zones, while maintaining data isolation. Rather than moving data to the model, bring the model to the data. By containerizing model inference and deploying it regionally, organizations can comply with data laws while maintaining global coverage. Regional tuning of models also improves accuracy, as behavior patterns vary significantly between countries. What's normal in Lagos might be suspicious in London. A fraud system that treats all activity the same way will either underperform or overflag, both of which are dangerous at scale.

But regionalization introduces another tension, balancing availability, consistency, and security. Distributed systems often rely on eventual consistency models to maintain performance across geographies. Yet in fraud detection, eventual is often too late. If one node flags a threat, but that insight isn't shared across regions fast enough, a coordinated attack can unfold before systems catch up. Engineers must architect for rapid replication of high-sensitivity signals ensuring that critical risk indicators propagate instantly, even if transactional data is synchronized later. This often involves a layered architecture, where high-priority security events are handled through dedicated, high-throughput channels, separate from standard data pipelines.

At scale, cross-border fraud becomes one of the hardest types to detect and prevent. Attackers exploit the blind spots between regions. A stolen credential used in one country may not look suspicious if the account was just accessed from another "valid" country seconds ago. If systems don't share behavioral baselines across regions, fraudsters can simulate distributed usage to mask intent. This is where geo-intelligent detection becomes critical.

Geo-intelligent systems don't just look at where a transaction is coming from. They look at how that location compares to typical behavior for the account, how long it's been since the last access, whether multiple geographies are being used simultaneously, and whether the network path matches the physical geography. They assess travel velocity could a user have realistically moved from one login point to another in that time? They evaluate device consistency was this same device seen in another country minutes ago? When combined, these signals form a profile that goes beyond geography. They reflect movement, intent, and coordination.

Some advanced systems integrate with telco providers and IP intelligence networks to verify not just location, but network trustworthiness. Is this an anonymized IP? A known proxy? A botnet node? Fraud detection at scale must tap into external threat intelligence, blending internal behavior analysis with signals from outside the perimeter. This helps teams move from reactive detection to anticipatory defense, identifying infrastructure known to support attacks before it ever reaches the application layer.

Scaling secure infrastructure is not about having the most tools, it's about using the right ones, in the right places, with the right boundaries. When those systems are designed to think geographically, react in real time, comply locally, and collaborate globally, they become more than scalable, they become trustworthy, intelligent, and ready for whatever comes next.

When fraud systems operate at scale, failure is not a possibility, it is a certainty. Something will go wrong. A node will fail, a pipeline will break, a model will produce an anomalous output, or a cloud region will go dark. The real test of security infrastructure isn't how rarely these things happen, it's how well the system responds when they do. This is where disaster recovery and incident resilience step in not as afterthoughts, but as architectural pillars.

In fraud detection, recovery time is measured in losses. A one-minute outage can create a floodgate for high-speed fraud attempts. A poorly managed incident can result in data corruption, regulatory violations, or irreversible customer loss. Systems must be built to self-heal, to reroute traffic, replay messages, failover inference engines, and rehydrate context in real time. Detection pipelines must be idempotent, allowing events to be replayed without triggering duplicates or inconsistencies. Logs must be immutable. Models must be version-controlled, with the ability to roll back gracefully if a new model version underperforms or misbehaves in production.

But resilience also depends on people. Teams need incident playbooks that are tested not just read. They must simulate attacks, rehearse escalations, and practice what to do when systems falter. The most secure fraud platforms aren't just technically hardened, they're operationally prepared. They assume failure, and they know how to adapt.

Another hidden pressure at scale is cost. Fraud detection at enterprise level is not cheap. Every additional layer of detection, logging, model monitoring, or storage adds to the infrastructure bill. Engineering teams often face a difficult balancing act between performance, precision, and cost-efficiency. Over-monitoring everything can create more alerts than value. Over-indexing on model complexity can lead to slow inference and ballooning compute bills. Underbuilding leads to exposure. This is where cost-conscious security design comes into play.

Smart systems use tiered detection, low-latency models for real-time screening, and deeper analysis for queued or suspicious events. They compress data for storage without losing fidelity. They tune model thresholds not just for risk, but for economic trade-offs: what is the cost of flagging one more transaction vs. the cost of letting it pass? They leverage spot instances, container auto-scaling, and regional workload distribution to optimize resource usage.

Cost isn't just a budget line, it's an architectural influence. Systems that respect both financial and technical limits are more likely to be sustainable in the long run. They force clarity: what are we monitoring, why, and what is the real value of that signal?

As the future of fraud detection unfolds, the infrastructure will become increasingly AI-native, not just with isolated ML models running in cloud VMs, but with fully orchestrated AI decision layers, real-time adaptation, and infrastructure that learns. Feature stores will be shared across teams, models will be auto-tuned via reinforcement learning, and versioning will be automated to detect drift without manual retraining cycles. Governance will be applied programmatically: systems that know when data is outdated, when bias has crept in, or when user privacy is at risk.

Edge-based AI inference will also grow in importance. In high-risk, high-latency environments like mobile money, retail terminals, or on-device banking apps, some detection must happen before data even hits the cloud. Lightweight models embedded at the edge will handle first-pass validation, reducing roundtrip delay while maintaining coverage. This distributed intelligence, where detection is layered across edge, cloud, and archive; creates depth. It doesn't rely on one place to see everything. It sees everywhere.

And as this vision unfolds, the role of leadership in scaling security becomes more strategic than ever. Technical ability is not enough. Leaders must guide teams to build with clarity, operate with trust, and scale with ethics. They must define what trade-offs are acceptable, what risks are tolerable, and how decisions are governed. They must partner across disciplines, engineering, compliance, finance, product and ensure that growth does not come at the expense of control.

Because in the end, scaling isn't just about supporting more users or handling more requests. It's about protecting more trust; trust that the system works, that the system watches, and that the system learns.

## Third-Party Integrations and the Supply Chain Risk at Scale

No cloud-native fraud detection system operates in isolation. As platforms scale, they inevitably integrate with third-party services; identity verification providers, payment gateways, cloud monitoring platforms, CRM systems, customer support tools, and third-party fraud scoring APIs. These integrations enable faster feature rollouts, smoother user experiences, and greater intelligence. But they also introduce a wide and often underestimated supply chain risk.

Each external service added to a financial system becomes a potential attack vector. A vulnerability in a partner's API, a compromised webhook, or a misconfigured permission setting in a third-party admin panel can open the door to exploitation despite the primary platform being technically secure. And because these services often sit between the platform and critical workflows like identity validation, KYC processing, or behavioral fingerprinting, their compromise can directly affect fraud detection outcomes.

For example, if a fraud model depends on third-party identity scores to make decisions, and that third party begins returning unreliable values due to internal error or manipulation, the fraud model's precision deteriorates instantly. Worse, if that dependency isn't monitored, no one might notice until real damage has been done. That's why dependency visibility is essential. Every external integration should be mapped, monitored, version-controlled, and tested regularly not just for uptime, but for trustworthiness.

Access control for third-party services must follow zero-trust principles. No integration should have access to more data than necessary. Each service should have its own scoped credentials, rotated frequently, with tightly logged API access. Critical workflows like onboarding, transaction authorization, or escalated fraud response should never rely on a single external provider without fallbacks. This redundancy is what separates robust fraud infrastructure from brittle ones.

Vendor evaluation also becomes more strategic at scale. It's not just about features or price, it's about their own security posture. Do they support audit logs? Do they offer data localization options? Are their AI decisions explainable? Do they undergo regular penetration testing? Choosing the wrong provider means inheriting their weaknesses. Scaling securely means partnering with those who protect as well as they perform.

## Maintaining Model Integrity in Complex Cloud Environments

The more sophisticated a fraud detection platform becomes, the more moving parts it contains and the harder it is to ensure that every model, every prediction, every decision remains valid, fair, and secure. In large-scale, cloud-native environments, **model integrity** is constantly at risk not because of malicious actors alone, but because of entropy: configuration drift, environment mismatch, data inconsistencies, or pipeline decay.

One of the most subtle dangers in scaled environments is silent model degradation. A model deployed six months ago may still run without throwing errors, but its performance could be declining due to new usage patterns, outdated feature mappings, or unseen shifts in user behavior. Without rigorous monitoring; drift detection, shadow deployment testing, continuous evaluation on fresh data, this degradation can remain invisible until false positives spike or fraud slips through.

Infrastructure complexity can also create integrity blind spots. If model inference is deployed across multiple regions or orchestrated via containerized services, differences in memory allocation, compute optimization, or software dependencies can lead to inconsistent outputs. The same input passed to the same model in two environments should produce the same result but in practice, differences in runtime versions, preprocessing logic, or environmental variables can introduce subtle inconsistencies.

This is why model governance must be treated with the same seriousness as source code governance. Each model version must be documented, reproducible, auditable, and tied to specific datasets. All training data must be stored in immutable archives for forensic backtesting. Serving infrastructure should include checksums, version tags, and output validators to detect divergence in behavior. Teams should use canary deployments and staged rollouts to validate new model versions under production pressure before full adoption.

Model explainability is also key to maintaining trust. At scale, it's not enough for the engineering team to understand why a transaction was flagged. That decision may be reviewed by compliance officers, customer service agents, or even regulators. Each model must provide decision traces, what features influenced the result, what thresholds were breached, and how confident the system was. This isn't just a debugging tool; it's a trust mechanism.

Finally, large-scale systems must also plan for model deprecation and retirement. No model lasts forever. As regulations change, user behavior evolves, or business priorities shift, some models will become outdated even if they technically still "work." Mature systems include lifecycle management: flagging models for review after a set period, archiving historical performance, and replacing legacy logic with more efficient or compliant alternatives. This keeps the system aligned not just with technology trends, but with organizational reality.

What makes a fraud detection system scalable isn't just that it handles more data, more users, or more transactions. It's that it scales with intention with governance, clarity, transparency, and trust. The cloud makes this possible. But only when the cloud is used thoughtfully, when infrastructure is designed to adapt, models are built to explain themselves, and third parties are selected with the same scrutiny as internal code.

As the world grows more connected, and fraud becomes more complex, this kind of intelligent infrastructure will no longer be a competitive edge, it will be the baseline. And those who get it right now, will be the ones others look to for the future.

# CHAPTER SIX
## DevSecOps in Financial Systems: Operationalizing AI-Powered Security at Scale

odern software engineering is fast. Agile cycles ship code weekly, sometimes daily. Infrastructure spins up and down with a few lines of configuration. Teams work across time zones, pushing updates into cloud environments where users transact, sign in, pay bills, and store sensitive data. In this environment, fraud detection systems can't afford to be reactive or bolted on. They must be baked into the fabric of development itself, living within the CI/CD pipeline, responding in real time, and adapting without slowing down delivery.

That's the promise of DevSecOps: a cultural and technical shift that merges development, security, and operations into a single continuous workflow. In financial systems, this isn't just a best practice, it's survival. When code changes impact how users authenticate, how data is encrypted, or how transactions flow, a delay in security response can result in real losses. DevSecOps ensures that every line of code, every containerized service, every deployment is inspected, scored, and fortified as it's built not after it's released.

In fraud prevention, this means integrating AI detection logic into the same systems that developers use to build features. Model updates aren't separate from deployments, they are deployments. New versions of a fraud scoring engine must be tested alongside new product features. Pipelines must support rollback of both application logic and machine learning weights. Monitoring must watch not only for technical errors but for risk impact shifts is a newly deployed feature increasing flagged transactions? Are false positives rising in a particular segment?

These signals must feed back into development. Just as performance regressions block releases, so too must security regressions. In a mature DevSecOps environment, security gates are applied automatically. Static analysis tools scan code for known vulnerabilities as it's written. Dependency scanners monitor libraries for threats introduced through open-source usage. Infrastructure-as-code templates are validated for misconfigurations, missing encryption, over-permissive access, hardcoded credentials. And all of it happens before merge, before deployment, and ideally, before humans have to intervene.

For AI-powered fraud systems, the stakes are even higher. The models themselves become part of the attack surface. If a model is trained on manipulated data, biased input, or adversarial samples, it can introduce systemic blind spots into the platform.

DevSecOps in this context means securing the entire ML lifecycle, from data collection to training pipelines to model deployment endpoints. Data must be validated. Feature engineering must be reproducible. Model artifacts must be signed and versioned. Inference endpoints must be monitored for abuse, and models must be tested for adversarial resilience.

But the value of DevSecOps goes beyond just safety. It improves feedback loops; the very thing AI systems rely on to evolve. When analysts flag a false positive, that data must flow back into the model training system. When fraud is detected manually, the related signals should be injected into feature engineering pipelines. This is how fraud systems become smarter not from weekly retraining, but from continuous learning loops built directly into development workflows.

In high-performing teams, this integration is seamless. Developers don't "call security", they work with it. Security reviews aren't last-minute meetings, they are embedded in pull request workflows. Feature flags allow new logic to be tested in isolation. Canary deployments enable models to be rolled out gradually, monitored under real traffic before full exposure. Metrics are shared. Logs are centralized. When something breaks or when something improves; everyone can see it, understand it, and act on it.

Of course, embedding this culture is not automatic. It requires commitment. It requires tools. But more importantly, it requires alignment. Developers must see security not as a blocker, but as a product enabler. Security teams must understand business goals and support innovation, not suppress it. Operations teams must optimize for resilience, not just uptime. And leadership must invest in automation, in observability, and in cross-functional rituals that bring these groups together.

In regulated industries like finance, DevSecOps also becomes a compliance strategy. Automated security checks, signed infrastructure changes, and audit-friendly logs make it easier to prove that standards are being followed. Instead of scrambling during audits, teams can present a living history of how software is built, deployed, and protected, on demand, with clarity.

At its best, DevSecOps turns security from a reactive function into a proactive advantage. It enables fraud detection systems to adapt as fast as the products they protect. It reduces the window between threat identification and defense. It creates a culture where secure software is not a goal, it's a byproduct of how things are done.

One of the most overlooked challenges in DevSecOps, particularly in organizations deploying AI-powered fraud detection is the disconnect between AI teams and software engineering teams. These teams often operate on different cadences, use different tools, and speak slightly different technical dialects. While engineering teams focus on reliability, scalability, and code quality, AI teams are immersed in experimentation, metrics tuning, and iterative learning. Bridging this gap is essential for fraud systems to become truly operational.

This alignment begins with shared infrastructure. When machine learning pipelines are treated as first-class citizens in CI/CD workflows, model updates can be versioned, tested, staged, and deployed just like application code. AI artifacts such as trained models, preprocessing logic, and validation thresholds are stored in secured registries. Deployment pipelines validate the compatibility of new models with real-time inference APIs, performance baselines, and compliance rules. This standardization not only improves reliability, it demystifies AI for engineering teams who must support it in production.

Security automation throughout the SDLC is what gives DevSecOps its real-time defense posture. It's not enough to scan the codebase once before release. Automated tools must run **continuously**, embedded in every stage of development. From the moment a developer initiates a feature branch, automated linters and static analysis tools should review code for insecure patterns. As builds compile, dependency checkers scan third-party libraries for known vulnerabilities. When infrastructure is provisioned, policy-as-code engines validate configurations against baseline security expectations: Is encryption enabled? Are ports locked? Is least privilege enforced?

These checks extend into the AI lifecycle. Before a new model is released, test suites validate its behavior under adversarial scenarios: what happens if the model is fed manipulated input? How does it respond to borderline cases? Can it be confused by minor variations in user activity? The goal isn't perfection, it's predictability. A secure AI system behaves consistently under pressure and fails gracefully when conditions fall outside known boundaries.

One of the most valuable practices in DevSecOps is shift-left testing, introducing security validation earlier in the development lifecycle. In fraud detection, this could mean simulating how new application features might be exploited by bad actors, even before code is written. For example, if a product team proposes a new peer-to-peer transfer feature, security teams should model how it could be misused to launder funds or circumvent limits. This foresight helps shape architecture decisions before flaws become systemic.

For AI models, shift-left means testing the integrity of the data pipeline at ingestion. Are data sources trustworthy? Are labels consistent and verified? Is the sampling representative of real-world use? Data poisoning when an attacker subtly corrupts training data to manipulate outcomes isn't always caught at the modeling phase. Prevention starts at the edge of the pipeline. And in DevSecOps environments, that edge is constantly monitored, verified, and tested.

After deployment, the job is far from over. Real-time observability becomes the next pillar of protection. Fraud detection systems must be monitored not just for availability, but for behavior. Are model predictions suddenly skewed toward false positives? Are transaction risk scores flattening across user segments? Has system latency increased under load? These questions require deep telemetry; logs, traces, metrics, and alerts stitched together across systems, centralized in a way that supports fast diagnosis.

Model monitoring platforms track accuracy, drift, and input anomalies over time. Security incident and event management (SIEM) systems aggregate logs from inference engines, user authentication services, and external threat feeds. When anomalies arise such as a spike in blocked logins from a particular geography, or a sudden drop in fraud detection sensitivity, alerts are triggered. In advanced systems, automated playbooks are launched: access tokens are revoked, model versions are rolled back, alert messages are escalated, and forensic data is collected for analysis.

This post-deployment observability does more than catch failures, it drives learning. Each anomaly becomes a lesson. Each incident becomes a training scenario. Each fraud attempt becomes a data point. In a DevSecOps culture, these lessons feed back into the development cycle. Sprint retrospectives include threat analysis. Roadmaps are informed by real attack patterns. The system evolves not just through code, but through **operational wisdom**.

What makes DevSecOps work in high-stakes, AI-driven environments is its cyclical nature. It's not a security phase tagged onto release day. It's a heartbeat; constant, responsive, embedded into every layer of design, testing, deployment, and feedback. It doesn't just make software more secure. It makes teams more aligned. And it makes platforms more prepared, not just for today's threats, but for tomorrow's uncertainty.

**Cultural Transformation:** Embedding Security Thinking Across Teams

No DevSecOps strategy succeeds on tooling alone. Tools automate, enforce, and accelerate but it is culture that determines adoption, ownership, and resilience. In many organizations, security remains an isolated discipline, a team that appears late in the process, flags concerns, and gets bypassed in the name of delivery speed. In high-stakes financial systems, this cultural silo is not just inefficient, it's dangerous.

Transforming this culture starts with a mindset shift: security is everyone's responsibility, not just that of the security engineers. Developers must understand how their code impacts the attack surface. Product managers must know how new features could be abused. Data scientists must consider how inputs can be manipulated or misused. Operations teams must know how to monitor not just infrastructure health, but security behavior. When security is framed as an enabling force, not a gatekeeper, it becomes easier to bring everyone to the table.

Embedding security into daily rituals is where culture takes root. Security discussions shouldn't be rare. They should be a part of backlog grooming, sprint planning, code reviews, and incident retrospectives. When a developer submits a pull request, the question should no longer be "Does it work?" but "Does it work securely?" When an AI team deploys a new model, the question should be "Does it make accurate predictions?" and "Can those predictions be abused?"

To support this mindset, training is essential. Secure coding practices must be taught and reinforced. Teams should be exposed to real-world breach case studies, internal threat simulations, and hands-on security challenges. Engineers should be given access to their own security telemetry so they can see what attackers see, and fix what attackers might exploit.

Psychological safety is just as important. Team members must feel empowered to report weaknesses, question decisions, and flag suspicious behaviors, without fear of blame. When people feel safe pointing out potential risks, those risks surface early. When they're afraid to speak, risks go underground until they're too big to contain. A secure culture is one where curiosity is rewarded, not punished.

Ultimately, cultural transformation happens through consistency. The more security becomes a part of the team's identity, their vocabulary, habits, and metrics, the less it feels like a burden and the more it becomes a shared source of pride. That's when DevSecOps becomes more than process, it becomes posture.

## AI Ethics and Secure Experimentation in DevSecOps

As financial institutions deploy more advanced AI systems to detect fraud, approve credit, and monitor behavior, the line between technical precision and ethical responsibility becomes razor thin. A high-performing AI model may reduce fraud by 40% but what if it does so by unfairly flagging users from a particular region? What if its training data excluded entire user groups, resulting in poor decisions for newcomers? What if its thresholds deny access to the financially underserved, reinforcing systemic inequality?

These aren't theoretical questions. They're real-world consequences of scaling AI without ethical guardrails. And in DevSecOps, where speed and automation reign, these risks can go unnoticed unless teams build ethics into experimentation.

Ethical AI in DevSecOps starts with intentional experimentation design. Before a new model is tested, teams must define what ethical success looks like: not just fraud reduction, but fairness, inclusion, and explainability. Experiments must be reviewed not only for performance metrics, but for demographic distribution, outlier handling, and impact on vulnerable users. If a model disproportionately flags transactions from certain device types or regions, that's not just a bug, it's a signal that bias may be present in the pipeline.

Secure experimentation also means protecting data integrity. In fast-moving DevSecOps cultures, it's easy to clone datasets for testing or create temporary data snapshots. But if those datasets contain financial information, personal identifiers, or behavior logs, they must be handled with the same rigor as production data. Data anonymization, encryption at rest, access logging, and fine-grained permissions must be enforced even in test environments.

Moreover, experimentation in fraud systems must be non-exploitative by design. A/B testing that exposes users to weaker fraud rules even temporarily can backfire catastrophically. Experiments must be structured with containment in mind. If a new model performs poorly, it must be easy to isolate, trace, and roll back without affecting production systems. Canary deployments, feature flag rollouts, and environment segmentation are not just conveniences, they are ethical safeguards.

AI ethics in DevSecOps is also about accountability. Who signed off on a model deployment? Who reviewed the experimental impact? Who owns the decision to retrain, reweight, or reclassify? These questions must have clear answers. Audit trails must link model changes to responsible individuals. Cross-functional committees, drawing from engineering, compliance, data science, and legal should review sensitive models on a recurring basis. When fraud systems make high-impact decisions, the chain of responsibility must be visible and defensible.

At the intersection of AI, security, and speed, DevSecOps is more than a technical practice, it is an ethical commitment. A commitment to protect users not only from external fraud, but from internal oversight. A commitment to build systems that adapt not just to threats, but to truth. A commitment to scale without losing sight of humanity.

# CHAPTER SEVEN
## Lessons from the Field: Real-World Case Studies in AI-Powered Financial Security

In the controlled world of whiteboards, documentation, and development sprints, it's easy to believe that a well-architected fraud system will behave exactly as intended. But the real world has a way of testing assumptions. In production environments where infrastructure shifts, customers behave unpredictably, and bad actors innovate constantly, theory is only a starting point. The real lessons are learned through failures, adaptations, and unexpected outcomes.

One early case involved a digital wallet platform operating across several West African countries. The engineering team had just rolled out an AI-powered fraud detection system trained on transaction behavior, velocity, and geolocation data. The model performed well in sandbox testing, flagging test cases with 92% accuracy. But within two weeks of going live, a new pattern emerged: coordinated fraudsters were exploiting a vulnerability in the registration process. By using rotating devices and spoofed locations, they bypassed identity checks, created fake accounts, and funneled microtransactions through multiple hops. The model missed them not because it was poorly built, but because it had never seen this particular behavior before.

The breakthrough came not from the model but from a support analyst who noticed a series of complaints from users receiving money they didn't expect. The engineering team dug into logs and discovered the pattern: low-value transfers bouncing between fake accounts and eventually pooling into a real one. The system was treating them as unrelated events. The fix wasn't just a model tweak, it required adding a graph analytics layer that could detect relational anomalies across accounts. Once deployed, the updated system not only blocked the fraud loop but revealed multiple smaller schemes previously hidden in transaction noise.

Another story comes from a fintech startup that launched a peer-to-peer lending platform. As the business grew, so did the risk. Fraudsters began applying for loans using synthetic identities, combining real data from leaked databases with fake profiles that passed basic checks. The company had an AI model in place that scored risk based on credit behavior and identity inputs. But the model had been trained on clean, well-structured data. In production, the incoming signals were messy, incomplete, and, in some cases, manipulated.

At first, fraud losses were treated as exceptions. But soon they became a pattern. The root issue? The model was over-reliant on structured identity fields like email, phone number, and government ID and underweighted behavioral signals. Once the fraud team added passive signals like typing speed, session time, device switching frequency, and social graph data from referral networks, the detection rate spiked. The takeaway was clear: synthetic identities can pass static tests but struggle with consistent behavior. Real people leave patterns. Fake ones leave friction.

In another case, a large regional bank had integrated an AI model into their customer onboarding flow. The goal was to score applicants in real time, reducing manual reviews and improving sign-up speed. The system worked well, until regulators requested an audit of decisions. That's when things got complicated. The model had been trained with no explainability layer. Risk scores were generated, but the reasons behind those scores weren't logged or exposed. When questioned about why certain applications were rejected, the bank couldn't give a defensible answer. It wasn't a fraud crisis, it was a transparency crisis.

The model wasn't biased, but the lack of interpretability created legal and reputational risk. The solution wasn't technical alone. It required retraining the model with explainable techniques, building an internal "reasoning engine" that could surface top contributing features, and overhauling the logging system to retain inference context for audit purposes. From then on, every decision carried metadata that explained itself not only to engineers but to users, regulators, and support teams. The bank learned that in finance, accuracy without accountability is a liability.

Some of the most powerful lessons come not from failure, but from careful prevention. One neobank deployed an intelligent feature gating system allowing fraud detection teams to roll out rule changes, threshold updates, and model versions independently of product code. This reduced coupling between fraud logic and feature velocity. When a coordinated phishing campaign hit users, the team was able to deploy updated behavioral scoring within hours, without waiting for an engineering sprint. The fraud impact was contained, and the product roadmap stayed on track. Their secret wasn't just good tooling, it was autonomy, ownership, and a culture of rapid, secure response.

But not every smart system works forever. In a high-volume payment gateway serving multiple countries, fraud rates suddenly spiked despite having layered AI models in place. Investigations revealed that fraudsters were training their own models, testing the platform with small transactions to map the detection thresholds. Over time, they learned how to mimic average behavior closely enough to blend in. The solution? Introducing randomized features and rotating detection models. By making the fraud system less predictable, the attackers lost their advantage. The lesson: if your detection logic becomes predictable, it becomes obsolete.

Across all these stories, one theme stands out: adaptation is everything. The most effective fraud detection systems aren't perfect, they're responsive. They don't prevent all attacks, they evolve with each one. They're not afraid of failure; they learn from it. And most importantly, they're built not just to protect transactions, but to protect trust in the system, in the company, and in the people using them.

In one particularly illuminating case, a digital-first remittance platform noticed an uptick in account takeovers. These weren't large-scale brute force attacks or phishing campaigns; they were subtle, precise, and highly targeted. Fraudsters were logging into dormant user accounts that hadn't seen activity in months and executing small transactions under the radar. Because these transactions fell within normal limits and were conducted using stored beneficiary information, most models flagged nothing. The system had learned to treat inactivity as low risk, an assumption that attackers exploited.

The fix wasn't to block inactive accounts. That would have disrupted thousands of genuine users. Instead, the team introduced time-aware behavioral modeling, assigning higher risk to transactions that occurred after long periods of user inactivity especially when combined with new device fingerprints or altered access patterns. The solution wasn't about punishing inactivity, but about contextualizing it within behavior dynamics. Once deployed, the model began catching subtle reactivation fraud, and over time, dormant account abuse nearly vanished.

A different kind of case came from a fast-scaling buy-now-pay-later (BNPL) provider that allowed users to shop across multiple partner platforms. As usage grew, so did fraud pressure but not in the way the company expected. Instead of direct payment fraud or fake identities, fraudsters began leveraging the refund system. They'd place orders, wait for partial deliveries or delays, and initiate refunds using complaint templates tailored to each merchant's process. The AI-powered fraud engine, trained on transactional and payment data, was blind to the refund abuse because it never touched that side of the pipeline.

The fraud operations team uncovered the issue during a manual investigation and quickly flagged it to engineering. But integrating refund signals into the fraud engine wasn't straightforward. Refund data came from partner platforms, arrived asynchronously, and often lacked structured formats. Still, the team persisted. They built connectors to ingest refund logs, normalized the data, and trained a separate model to detect patterned refund abuse. Over time, this model helped reduce refund fraud losses by over 40%, and the organization learned a vital lesson: fraud doesn't always happen at the point of payment, it thrives in the gaps between systems.

Yet another case unfolded within a cross-border microfinance platform that offered mobile credit to underserved populations. Their fraud model worked well in urban markets where device patterns, network reliability, and identity verification were relatively stable. But when the platform expanded into remote regions, false positives surged. Devices were shared between family members, SIM cards rotated frequently, and GPS data became unreliable. The model, designed for structured digital behavior, failed in environments where digital signals were noisy or nonlinear.

Rather than retrain the model blindly, the team initiated region-specific behavioral baselining. They stopped comparing rural behavior to global norms and instead began learning what "normal" looked like in each community. Risk scoring became hyper-local. A shared phone number was no longer a fraud signal, it was a socioeconomic pattern. A four-day delay in repaying credit wasn't a breach, it was consistent with market cash flow. As a result, fraud detection became more accurate, default rates fell, and customer trust improved. The key shift wasn't technical, it was empathetic calibration, an understanding that digital behavior is shaped by local context, not global averages.

One of the most thought-provoking stories came from a mature financial institution that had implemented AI-based risk scoring for high-value B2B transfers. The model used transaction metadata, client history, and recipient behavior to flag unusual activity. But during an internal audit, the team discovered that high-value transactions from long-standing clients were **never** flagged. The model had implicitly learned to trust tenure over behavior, believing that older clients posed less risk. Unfortunately, a fraud ring had also figured this out and began compromising dormant corporate accounts, issuing high-value transfers under the radar.

The issue wasn't that the model was poorly trained. It was that no one questioned the implicit trust assumptions baked into the feature weighting. When the team reweighted for behavioral deviation instead of tenure bias, the model began surfacing dormant corporate account activity more aggressively. This case reinforced a subtle truth: in AI systems, bias doesn't always show up in the data, it often hides in what the team forgets to challenge.

Across these cases, one thread emerges repeatedly: fraud adapts to assumptions. It thrives in blind spots between systems, within defaults, beneath thresholds. AI-powered fraud systems don't fail because they aren't smart, they fail when the humans building them forget to keep asking hard questions. "What aren't we seeing?" "What behavior are we normalizing that attackers could mimic?" "What decisions are we automating without review?"

And this is the real value of case studies not to celebrate the wins alone, but to show how teams recover from near-misses, how models are humbled and rebuilt, and how detection evolves not just through data, but through insight.

## Case Study One: Scaling Trust Across Ecosystems — Lessons from a Cross-Platform API Attack

The story begins with a fintech platform that had grown rapidly in less than three years, offering digital wallets, merchant APIs, microloans, and a developer sandbox that enabled third-party startups to integrate with its payment rails. By all external measures, the company was thriving. Partnerships with regional banks flourished, API documentation was clean and well-maintained, and fraud detection engines built with AI from the start, handled the consumer side effectively.

But trouble wasn't brewing at the login screen. It was hiding in the API layer, where thousands of daily requests poured in from third-party partners, legitimate fintechs building on top of the platform's infrastructure. These partners were given scoped API keys, rate limits, and documentation. But what the fraud team didn't anticipate was that one small startup, which had integrated with the platform months ago and barely transacted, would become the doorway to a slow, calculated data siphon.

It started with a low-level anomaly, a spike in 200 OK responses from a partner whose traffic was previously negligible. At first, the activity seemed harmless: balance checks, transaction histories, user metadata fetches. But when mapped chronologically, a disturbing pattern emerged. The API calls were being chained, using balance responses from one user to simulate inquiries for another, bouncing across endpoints in what the team later called a logic loop.

The attacker hadn't breached credentials. They were exploiting a flaw in how rate limits were applied. Because the fraud system prioritized payment events and transactional anomalies, it had no mechanism for analyzing non-financial API behavior. The attacker's requests were legal, sequential, and passed all authentication. But the pattern was unnatural. No real integration would behave that way. It wasn't until the logs were replayed through a behavior profiler, typically used for mobile session analysis that the abnormality became clear.

This led the team to build a secondary AI pipeline, focused entirely on API usage modeling. Unlike transaction scoring, this model used request intervals, endpoint sequences, metadata field reuse, and signature entropy to score partners not users for risk. It flagged the offending account within days. But the bigger lesson was architectural: trusting the edge especially in developer platforms requires more than authentication. It requires behavioral observability on every interaction, financial or not.

Just as the API issue began to settle, another form of fraud surfaced, one that couldn't be modeled through machine learning alone. A junior support engineer, with scoped access to refund workflows and transaction override tools, began issuing micro-refunds to accounts he created himself. Each refund was below the internal threshold for supervisor review. Each one was documented properly, with fake complaint tickets attached. Individually, the events seemed legitimate. But over several months, the amounts added up, quietly funneling funds into external wallets.

This time, the fraud model flagged nothing. It wasn't trained to correlate HR records with platform activity. It didn't have access to staff workflow logs. And even if it did, it lacked the context to know that repeated action across multiple departments was unusual for an entry-level support role.

The breach came to light during a routine audit but the response was transformative. The engineering and security teams introduced a cross-domain anomaly detection system, blending fraud signals with internal logs, admin tool usage, access patterns, and even time-based role-behavior matching. What emerged wasn't just a tighter fraud system. It was a trust architecture, one that treated internal users with the same scrutiny as external attackers, not from suspicion, but from principle: trust must be verifiable, even inside your own walls.

In the end, both attacks; one external, one internal reminded the organization that fraud doesn't always come crashing through the front door. Sometimes it walks in quietly through trusted channels, speaking the language of normalcy. And only when systems are designed to question that normalcy through visibility, adaptability, and humility can they remain truly secure at scale.

## Case Study Two: When Good Intentions Break the System — Behavioral Drift in a Lending App

The consumer credit space thrives on precision, who to trust, how much to lend, when to flag misuse. And for one mobile-first lending platform operating across three African countries, AI was the golden ticket. From day one, machine learning models powered everything: credit scoring, disbursement velocity, repayment reminders, and fraud detection.

The app's early success hinged on a simple, elegant risk engine. It scored users based on device signals, repayment history, contact graph analysis, and transaction activity. For the first 18 months, it worked beautifully; fraud was low, repayment was high, and the model kept pace with the company's rapid expansion.

Until it didn't.

The breaking point wasn't a hack, breach, or model failure. It was scale. As the platform launched a referral bonus system, a new pattern emerged: clusters of users began signing up with similar device profiles, similar contact lists, and nearly identical repayment behavior. At first, the fraud team celebrated, more signups, more repayments, more activity.

But buried in that activity was a slow bleed. Users had discovered that by creating micro-variations of their identity across SIM cards and devices, they could refer themselves, draw credit, repay it quickly, and repeat. No rule was being technically violated. But the system, designed for authentic organic growth, was now fueling synthetic circular behavior.

The AI model, however, had no reason to panic. These users paid on time. Their devices were clean. And because their repayment behavior matched the platform's "ideal borrower" profile, their credit limits kept increasing. By the time the anomaly was spotted through an unexpected dip in new-customer default rates, the platform had disbursed over $400,000 to accounts created by fewer than 600 individuals.

The fix wasn't just about tightening verification. That had already been done. What changed was the philosophy: the team began modeling not just what users were doing, but why they were doing it. They added intent signals: referral rate velocity, contact graph overlap, time-of-day borrowing consistency, and even the ratio of repayment-to-borrow timing. This allowed the system to detect orchestrated behavior without punishing legitimate users who simply paid on time.

The team also throttled the growth loop, introducing a tiered bonus delay, fraud-aware referral caps, and additional behavioral triggers. Borrowing volume stabilized, defaults dropped, and most importantly, the fraud system began to see what it previously missed: patterns of opportunity abuse camouflaged as growth.

While solving that issue, a second problem surfaced; one from the opposite end of the risk spectrum. In its attempt to reduce default rates, the fraud detection engine began aggressively flagging new users with inconsistent data. If a user borrowed money from a low-data device, or if their repayment channel differed from their initial onboarding location, they were immediately classified as high risk.

But in many of the platform's rural regions, these behaviors weren't fraud; they were normal. Families shared phones. Agents processed repayments on behalf of users. And location mismatches were common due to fluctuating network coverage. The fraud system had learned its patterns well but not its context.

Complaints started to rise. Users were confused, agents were overwhelmed, and customer trust began to erode. What began as a system designed to protect people was now misunderstanding them.

So, the team did something radical: they paused model updates. For one sprint cycle, no new weights were pushed. Instead, they initiated a feedback roundtable, pulling in field agents, customer support staff, and loan officers. They listened. They annotated misclassified sessions. They rewrote the labeling logic. And most importantly, they retrained the model with more empathy.

The result? A detection engine that didn't just score for risk, but for environmental flexibility. It learned that intent and behavior aren't always linear and that sometimes, anomalies aren't malicious. They're just human.

By blending AI power with human nuance, the team rebalanced their system not towards leniency, but towards fairness. And in doing so, they preserved what mattered most: trust in a system built to serve, not just secure.

# CHAPTER EIGHT
## Compliance, Governance, and Ethical Intelligence in Financial AI Systems

In the financial world, building secure systems isn't enough, they must also be **compliant, explainable, and auditable**. While machine learning and AI have brought unprecedented sophistication to fraud prevention, they've also introduced a new class of risks: invisible logic, unpredictable edge cases, and decisions that can't always be traced by the very people responsible for them. At scale, these risks aren't just technical, they're legal, ethical, and reputational.

Financial systems sit at the intersection of regulation and real-time response. Every decision an AI model makes whether it blocks a transaction, denies a loan, or flags a user has consequences that ripple across businesses and individual lives. Unlike e-commerce or social platforms, where misjudgments might lead to inconvenience, errors in financial decision-making can trigger financial exclusion, regulatory violations, and legal disputes. That's why compliance isn't just a box to check, it's a mindset embedded in design, deployment, and daily operations.

The challenge is that traditional compliance frameworks weren't built for AI. They assume static systems with clearly documented decision paths. But AI models learn, evolve, and infer, often without explicitly stated logic. This creates a conflict between the nature of intelligence and the need for transparency. A model might be 97% accurate, but if a regulator asks why a transaction was flagged, "The model said so" isn't a valid answer. And when audits come whether from internal teams, external regulators, or public scrutiny, organizations must be able to trace, explain, and justify every significant decision the system makes.

This is where AI governance begins not just as documentation, but as intentional architecture. From the moment a model is conceived, teams must define what "acceptable behavior" looks like: What data can it access? What attributes should be excluded to prevent bias? How will its predictions be logged? What thresholds require human review? Governance frameworks ensure that these questions are not afterthoughts but requirements woven into the build process.

Logging and traceability become vital. Every decision made by a fraud detection engine must be attached to context what features contributed, what risk level was assigned, what version of the model was used, and who deployed it. These logs don't just enable debugging, they become evidence. In regulated environments, the ability to show "why" is often more important than showing "what." A slightly less accurate model that explains itself is often more valuable than a black-box system that leaves no trail.

Fairness is another pillar. AI models are reflections of their training data, and in finance, that data often contains historical bias. If certain communities have faced systemic barriers to financial access, models trained on historical outcomes may learn to deny them opportunities again. This feedback loop where AI amplifies past exclusion poses one of the most insidious risks in financial systems. Teams must audit models not just for performance, but for impact across demographics, geographies, and user segments.

To address this, responsible AI development includes fairness testing and bias mitigation. Before deployment, models are stress-tested on synthetic inputs that simulate edge cases, minority behaviors, and alternative data structures. Model outputs are reviewed not just for correctness, but for disparity. Metrics like equal opportunity, demographic parity, and disparate impact are calculated and monitored, ensuring that fraud detection doesn't unintentionally punish users for being different.

Privacy is equally critical. AI-powered fraud detection often relies on behavior analytics, device telemetry, geolocation, and identity markers. While powerful, these inputs must be collected, processed, and stored in accordance with privacy laws and user consent. Regulations like GDPR, CCPA, and emerging African data protection laws require not just consent mechanisms, but data minimization, user access rights, and the right to explanation. This means engineering systems that can answer user questions like:

"What data do you have on me?" or "Why was I flagged?", quickly, clearly, and respectfully.

AI governance also includes access control, who can see model outputs, who can update thresholds, who can retrain pipelines. Not every team member should have access to fraud decision logs or user identity clusters. Access must be role-based, logged, and time-bound. And when changes are made to the system, those changes must pass through review, testing, and compliance checks because in fraud systems, even a small update can change how risk is measured and money is moved.

But perhaps the most overlooked aspect of governance is incident response. What happens when the system gets it wrong? When users are blocked unfairly, or fraud slips through, how is accountability handled? Governance includes escalation policies, customer resolution flows, and feedback loops that allow wrong decisions to be corrected without destroying trust. The best systems aren't the ones that never fail, they're the ones that fail transparently, recover gracefully, and learn continuously.

In fast-moving environments, some teams fear that governance will slow innovation. But the opposite is often true. When security, compliance, and ethical requirements are codified into pipelines via automation, documentation, and feedback loops, they accelerate decision-making. Teams move faster because they're not guessing. Risks are known, limits are clear, and standards are shared.

In the race to outsmart fraudsters, it's tempting to build fast and ask questions later. But in finance, where trust is currency, compliance is not optional. It's a form of design. It's a promise to users, partners, regulators, and society that innovation will not come at the cost of integrity.

For fintechs operating across Africa, Europe, and North America, this often means reconciling different expectations around data retention, AI accountability, and user rights. In Nigeria, for instance, the Nigeria Data Protection Regulation (NDPR) emphasizes consent and data minimization, while in the EU, GDPR goes further demanding explainability, user access to data, and clear lawful grounds for every automated decision. Meanwhile, emerging U.S. regulations in the financial services space lean toward sector-specific compliance, focusing on reporting requirements and bias mitigation in AI use.

The operational impact is significant. Fraud detection systems must now be geo-aware, not just in their scoring models, but in how data is stored, processed, and audited. User data collected in Lagos may need to be housed separately from data in Frankfurt or Toronto. Model behavior that's acceptable in one region must be retrained or reweighted in another to meet local definitions of fairness. Teams must build dynamic pipelines, ones that adapt policy, threshold, or inference behavior based on geography, regulatory versioning, and user segmentation.

This is where third-party audits enter the picture. No matter how ethical or transparent a team claims to be, external validation is increasingly becoming the standard. Regulatory bodies, investors, and business partners now demand independent review of fraud models especially those handling high-volume financial decisions. These audits go beyond pen-testing and code review. They evaluate model governance, decision traceability, explainability infrastructure, and bias mitigation processes.

A third-party audit might review how a model was trained, whether training data was diverse, whether audit trails are immutable, and whether human oversight is meaningfully present. They test how well the organization can respond to edge cases and whether the system can defend its decisions in a court of law or public opinion. For teams that build fast, these reviews can be uncomfortable, but they're powerful. Done right, they become **a mirror**: reflecting both the system's strengths and the blind spots no internal team could catch alone.

But beyond legality lies a more subtle frontier: the ethics of automation. As AI takes over more decision-making in fraud systems, we inch closer to a reality where algorithms determine financial inclusion, exclusion, and escalation, without human involvement. While this offers scale and efficiency, it also raises deep ethical questions: When should humans intervene? What thresholds require review? Should models ever have the final say in high-risk decisions like account closure, loan denial, or payment blocking?

The answer isn't simple. In low-stakes scenarios like flagging a password reset attempt, automation makes sense. But in high-impact decisions, automated outcomes must always be accompanied by accountability mechanisms. Users need channels to appeal. Systems must escalate ambiguous cases to human analysts. And every automated response should be stored with enough context to support investigation, reversal, or refinement.

This becomes especially important in edge cases. Consider a legitimate user who borrows a relative's device to complete a transaction. The fraud system, trained to spot device changes as high risk, flags the action and freezes the account. The user now faces disruption, embarrassment, or even financial harm. If there's no escalation path, no human review then automation has failed, not because of its model, but because of how rigidly it was enforced.

To balance speed with empathy, modern systems are beginning to integrate confidence scoring and intervention thresholds. If a model is 99% confident in its prediction, it may proceed with automation. But if confidence drops below a set point, or if certain risk flags overlap, the system holds action and routes it for human analysis. This allows for hybrid decision-making, where AI and human judgment collaborate rather than compete. And it reminds users that while technology is efficient, people are still listening.

That listening is, in the end, what sustains user trust. Users understand that fraud prevention exists to protect them but they also expect fairness, transparency, and recourse. A system that blocks suspicious activity but explains why, provides recovery steps, and supports real-time resolution earns more trust than one that acts invisibly. Design plays a major role here: how alerts are written, how escalation works, how clearly users can understand their next step. This isn't just CX. It's ethical UX, and in fraud systems, it's part of the product itself.

The best fraud systems don't just stop crime. They stop it while keeping trust intact. They scale across borders while adapting to local expectations. They build fast, but leave room for reflection. And most of all, they treat governance not as a constraint but as the blueprint for building something that lasts.

## From Black Box to Glass Box: Designing for Explainability from Day One

One of the most persistent fears surrounding AI in finance is its opacity. Fraud detection models, particularly deep learning systems are notorious for making accurate predictions without offering insight into how those predictions were made. In other sectors, this might be tolerable. But in financial software, decisions without explanation are decisions without legitimacy.

Explainability is no longer optional. Regulators demand it, users expect it, and businesses need it to defend high-impact outcomes. But achieving explainability after deployment is difficult and often superficial. Teams bolt on dashboards, expose a few feature weights, or simplify decision trees without truly illuminating how the model functions under pressure. This isn't real transparency, it's just enough visibility to reduce discomfort.

Real explainability must be designed into the system from day one. This means choosing algorithms and architectures that balance performance with interpretability. It also means enforcing design constraints that document why features are chosen, how labels are derived, and how the model behaves under stress. Tools like SHAP (SHapley Additive exPlanations), LIME (Local Interpretable Model-agnostic Explanations), and attention visualizations should be integrated into model pipelines not treated as afterthoughts.

Moreover, explainability is not just for auditors or engineers. It's for customer success teams, compliance officers, and frontline support agents who need to tell a user why their transaction was delayed or why their account was flagged. The system should surface clear, non-technical reasons. "Your payment was flagged because of a new device and unusual transfer location" not obscure metrics like anomaly scores or embeddings. This is the shift from black box to glass box systems; engines that are not only accurate, but understandable, inspectable, and ultimately, accountable.

The best fraud models are not the ones that predict best in a vacuum. They are the ones that invite scrutiny, evolve under oversight, and help everyone around them get smarter. Transparency, when done right, doesn't weaken security, it strengthens it by aligning human insight with machine judgment.

# Building Organizational Integrity Through AI Governance

Compliance, ethics, fairness, all these principles sound noble, but they only come alive when they are shared across the organization. It's easy to draft an AI governance policy or write a fairness memo. The real challenge is making it matter, embedding governance into the organizational fabric so that every team, not just security or legal, feels responsible for how AI decisions are made and managed.

This starts with leadership. When executives treat ethical AI as a business risk, not just a PR issue, priorities shift. Budgets open up. Hiring decisions change. Cross-functional teams are formed. Governance moves from a checklist to a core value. Product managers begin asking about model bias. Engineers think twice about default thresholds. Customer teams escalate fairness concerns. A culture of integrity emerges not because of mandates, but because people are watching, learning, and holding themselves to a higher standard.

Internal policy alone isn't enough. Organizations must also invest in AI governance infrastructure. This includes model registries with approval workflows, real-time compliance dashboards, automatic documentation generation, version control for both models and their data, and feedback loops that let users report issues with AI behavior. Governance should be felt as a presence, not a bottleneck, guiding decisions in real time rather than waiting until review cycles.

Accountability must also be clearly assigned. Who owns fairness audits? Who is responsible for retraining schedules? Who signs off on risk thresholds? Without names and roles attached, responsibility becomes invisible and invisible responsibility is a threat to integrity. Governance doesn't just protect users. It protects the company's credibility, and in financial services, credibility is the foundation of trust.

At its most powerful, organizational AI governance becomes an engine for innovation. By defining clear ethical boundaries and robust operational systems, teams are freed to build faster, confident that their ideas will scale without unraveling under legal, ethical, or social scrutiny. Governance becomes not a brake on progress, but the road itself, paved, measured, and aligned toward impact.

# CHAPTER NINE
## From Detection to Defense: Real-Time Threat Response in AI-Powered Fraud Systems

Fraud detection is no longer enough. As attack surfaces expand and adversaries move faster, financial software must shift from spotting threats to responding to them, instantly, intelligently, and without human bottlenecks. In this new paradigm, AI doesn't just label anomalies. It takes action. It freezes accounts, revokes tokens, alerts compliance teams, blocks transactions midstream, and escalates threats as they unfold not after the damage is done.

This is the evolution from static fraud monitoring to real-time threat response, a shift that transforms how financial platforms are built, how risk is measured, and how trust is preserved at scale.

The promise of real-time response begins with automation. In the past, fraud alerts often triggered manual review queues. Analysts would sift through flags, prioritize queues, and make decisions hours or even days after an event occurred. This worked when fraud was slow, when money moved in batches, and when user behavior followed predictable cycles. But today, transactions are instant. Money moves across borders in seconds. And fraud rings operate with algorithmic precision, testing systems at machine speed.

In this landscape, delays are fatal. The goal is no longer to review suspicious events, it's to intercept them before they settle. That's why modern systems are embedding AI into the decision path itself. When a transaction enters the pipeline, it's scored in real time, compared against behavioral baselines, and routed through decision layers that can take action within milliseconds. High-risk transactions are blocked. Suspicious sessions are throttled or verified through multi-step authentication. Risk signals are fed forward to other systems; device management, customer support, compliance dashboards, creating a coordinated response fabric.

But action alone isn't enough. Autonomous fraud response must be smart, explainable, and recoverable. Users can tolerate friction, what they can't tolerate is silent failure. If a payment is blocked, they need to know why, and what to do next. If an account is frozen, the system must offer resolution, not just restriction. This is where real-time response meets human-centered design. Systems must not only act, they must communicate, guide, and learn.

Behind the scenes, this responsiveness is made possible by event-driven architecture. Every significant action; login, transfer, device switch, location change is treated as an event, streamed through processing engines that evaluate context, score risk, and trigger outcomes. Instead of waiting for batch jobs or nightly reconciliation, systems now run as living flows, adjusting to each input with contextual memory and predictive foresight.

One key enabler of this model is the use of micro-decisions; small, modular logic blocks that evaluate individual risk dimensions. Instead of relying on a monolithic fraud score, systems assess device trustworthiness, transaction amount, timing, velocity, and behavioral deviation independently, then combine those insights to generate a composite decision. This allows for nuance: the same amount sent from a new device at 3 a.m. in one region might be flagged, while the same action from a verified device with clean history may pass unchallenged.

What's more, response systems are increasingly using feedback loops to learn in real time. When a user confirms a blocked action was valid, the system adjusts. When an analyst clears a false positive, that insight is captured and reflected in model weights. These continuous improvement cycles ensure that real-time action doesn't lead to rigidity. The system gets better, faster, and more aligned with both risk and reality.

Importantly, not all responses must be severe. Sometimes, the smartest move is to introduce adaptive friction. Instead of blocking a transaction, the system might pause it momentarily and ask for step-up verification. Instead of locking an account, it might send a behavioral challenge or location confirmation. These subtle defenses allow legitimate users to prove themselves while quietly discouraging malicious activity. In this way, the system becomes not just a wall but a gatekeeper, balancing protection with flow.

As threat response becomes more autonomous, systems must also account for blast radius. A false positive at scale doesn't just inconvenience a few users, it can trigger mass disruption, legal scrutiny, and reputational damage. That's why every response flow must be auditable, testable, and reversible. Before a model takes action, its logic must be validated. Before thresholds are adjusted, simulations must run. And when things go wrong as they inevitably will, teams must be able to explain, unwind, and improve the logic without panic.

Real-time fraud response isn't about replacing humans, it's about elevating them. Analysts are no longer burdened with triage. They become investigators, architects, and strategists focusing on edge cases, adversarial behavior, and system refinement. Their work becomes more meaningful, more proactive, and more creative.

As fraud response systems mature, their power lies not only in speed, but in synchronization. It's not enough to detect a threat in one place and act in isolation. In modern financial ecosystems, where users operate across mobile apps, web platforms, third-party integrations, and agent-assisted interfaces, response must be multi-channel and real-time. A flagged login on the web should inform mobile behavior. A blocked transaction on the app should update the call center agent's dashboard in seconds. This is fraud signal propagation and it's what turns individual detections into coordinated defenses.

Too often, detection is siloed. A model flags a transaction in one service, but that insight doesn't reach the fraud rules engine controlling another. As a result, threats slip through cracks not because they were undetected, but because the information wasn't shared in time. High-performing systems solve this with centralized event buses where all detection events, regardless of source, are streamed into a unified intelligence layer. This shared state becomes the foundation for decisions across the enterprise.

Imagine a customer's account behavior changes, an uncharacteristic device login, followed by a high-value transfer, and then a password reset request. In isolation, each event might pass. But seen together within a few seconds, they indicate potential compromise. Real-time systems correlate these fragments, escalate risk instantly, and take decisive but calibrated action: block the transaction, alert the user, verify identity. And they do it across touchpoints; email, SMS, in-app push because fraud doesn't wait, and trust demands immediacy.

Yet no system, no matter how advanced, can anticipate every scenario. Models can be manipulated, thresholds can be gamed, and automated decisions can cause unintended harm. That's why resilience in threat response isn't just about being right, it's about recovering well when wrong.

Every autonomous decision must have a recovery path. If a user is blocked in error, how fast can they regain access? If a system isolates funds, what's the resolution window? If an alert triggers a false compliance report, who intervenes? These aren't hypothetical questions; they are the reputational pressure points that shape user perception and regulatory scrutiny.

This is where failover strategies and guardrails matter. AI-powered systems should operate with tiered confidence zones. High-confidence fraud actions can trigger full automation. Medium-confidence scenarios may require dual-pathing: flagging the user for verification while allowing a manual override. Low-confidence cases should escalate to analysts before action. This triaging isn't a concession to inefficiency, it's an architecture of graceful fallback. Because speed without reversibility is just recklessness.

In some systems, the smartest move isn't to block, it's to contain. Rather than outright denial, advanced platforms use sandboxing techniques. A suspicious user may be allowed to log in, but with limited features. Transfers may be capped. Certain interactions may trigger silent secondary authentication flows. This containment **approach** protects against loss while reducing false positives. It gives users the benefit of doubt, while preserving infrastructure from exploitation.

The beauty of containment lies in its invisibility. Users aren't slammed with red alerts; they're subtly guided through flows that both secure the system and test legitimacy. Fraudsters, on the other hand, find their options limited, their scripts ineffective, and their efforts time-wasting. Over time, this friction becomes a deterrent and more importantly, a learning layer. Every contained session becomes data: improving future detection, refining thresholds, and reducing reliance on binary decisions.

The best threat response systems don't panic. They adapt. They scale intelligence across regions, products, and platforms. They distinguish between risk and routine, between anomaly and error. They empower humans to intervene when nuance is required, and they empower machines to act where speed is vital.

## Human-in-the-Loop Design for High-Stakes Decisions

For all the power that AI-driven automation brings to threat response, there remain moments where human intuition, context, and judgment are irreplaceable. While AI excels at pattern recognition, speed, and statistical confidence, it can falter in rare events, emotionally charged edge cases, or ambiguous intent. This is where human-in-the-loop (HITL) systems become essential, ensuring that high-impact decisions pass through human review before final execution.

Consider a scenario where a long-time corporate customer suddenly initiates a large cross-border transfer from a new device and location. The transaction matches some fraud signals, but also aligns with legitimate business behavior. Should the system block it? Delay it? Let it through? In these moments, HITL design kicks in. The AI system flags the risk, attaches context, suggests likely outcomes and then passes the case to a trained analyst for verification.

What makes HITL effective is not just that a human intervenes, but that the system is built to support that intervention. It provides clear evidence: model scores, historical behavior, geolocation mismatches, past alerts. It surfaces not only what the model sees, but how it came to its conclusion. The analyst isn't starting from scratch, they're working alongside the machine, combining speed with sense-making.

In well-designed HITL systems, feedback flows both ways. The analyst's override or approval becomes a learning signal for future model iterations. This reinforces a virtuous loop where the system grows more precise, the analyst grows more confident, and the decisions become sharper over time.

Critically, HITL must also respect workload and cognitive load. Analysts can't review everything, and not all decisions merit escalation. That's why mature systems incorporate tiered response models, ensuring that only the most uncertain, high-stakes, or user-sensitive cases reach human hands. Everything else is confidently and explainably handled by the AI, with logs for traceability and pathways for appeal if needed.

This partnership between automation and human intelligence is not just a safety net, it's a differentiator. In the financial services world, where trust is as important as throughput, knowing that the system includes a human conscience gives users and regulators, reassurance that the machine is not operating alone in a vacuum.

## Scaling Threat Response Without Compromising Customer Experience

One of the quiet dangers of scaling fraud response is the temptation to prioritize protection at the expense of experience. But financial systems exist to serve people, not to police them. If every login feels like an interrogation, if every transaction is a hurdle, users will lose patience, regardless of how secure the platform is. And worse, they may begin to feel criminalized by the very systems meant to protect them.

This is why experience-aware threat response must be a core pillar of any AI-driven fraud architecture. At scale, decisions must be fast but also friction-calibrated. Not every flag should result in a block. Not every anomaly should trigger a red screen. Instead, modern systems introduce graduated intervention, varying the level of user challenge based on risk, intent, and historical behavior.

For example, a low-risk flag might simply trigger passive monitoring or backend logging. A moderate-risk event might request device verification. A high-risk action may prompt real-time 2FA or short-term access suspension with a clear recovery path. What matters is that responses feel proportionate, not punitive.

Clarity is equally important. If a user's transaction is declined, the system should explain not in vague terms, but with friendly, actionable language. "We noticed something different about your login. Please confirm your device to proceed." Not: "Error 403:

Access denied." These small moments shape perception. They define whether users feel protected or punished.

Moreover, smart fraud systems consider the emotional state of the user. A blocked card during travel. A delayed payroll deposit. A suspended account during a business-critical transaction. These are moments where poor UX compounds frustration. The best platforms preempt this by offering clear timelines, fast escalation channels, and empathetic resolution flows.

And as fraud models get more complex, it becomes even more important to test them from a user journey perspective. Do changes in detection logic create false alerts during login surges? Do thresholds trigger blocks for new users unfamiliar with app flows? Are mobile-first users being unfairly penalized due to device constraints? These are not hypothetical issues, they're the subtle ways that fraud systems, when misaligned, degrade experience and erode loyalty.

Ultimately, the goal is not just to detect fraud but to do it in a way that users barely notice, except when it matters most. It's the difference between a system that feels like a barrier and one that feels like a guardian; quiet, responsive, respectful, and always on.

# CHAPTER TEN
## The Road Ahead: Designing for Security, Speed, and Resilience in the Next Era

The future of financial software will not be written in quarterly roadmaps or isolated innovation sprints. It will be forged in real time shaped by adversaries who move faster, users who expect more, and regulators who demand clarity. In this future, secure software engineering is no longer a specialization. It's a core discipline, a shared language across development, data science, product, and leadership. And its most important feature won't be complexity, it will be resilience.

In the coming years, fraud will evolve faster than most teams can imagine. Attackers are already leveraging generative AI to spoof voices, forge documents, and automate credential stuffing campaigns. Deepfakes will blur identity. Synthetic data will pollute training pipelines. Compromise will become more psychological; less about breaking systems and more about bending trust.

This means software engineers can't just code against yesterday's threats. They must build systems that expect change, systems that question assumptions, and systems that monitor themselves as closely as they monitor their users. It's not enough to detect anomalies, fraud engines must detect shifts in the definition of normal. Models must be retrainable, not just scalable. Features must be interpretable, not just effective. The next wave of secure systems won't just react, they'll adapt before the threat arrives.

But adaptability alone isn't enough. As AI gets stronger, so too must our ethical foundations. A system that defends well but discriminates quietly is still broken. A fraud engine that protects the platform but locks out legitimate users is still a liability. In the next era, leaders must hold their systems to higher standards not just in precision, but in accountability, fairness, and empathy.

Compliance will also evolve. New legislation will demand real-time explainability. Financial audits will extend to AI pipelines. Cross-border data residency rules will require dynamic infrastructure. And as central banks digitize currencies and governments introduce AI standards, the line between code and policy will blur. Engineers will become legal interpreters. Product managers will become risk architects. And teams will need tooling that bridges the gap between innovation and governance not after the fact, but by design.

At the same time, user expectations will rise. In a world of instant payments and invisible fintech, users will no longer tolerate delays, confusion, or silence. When something is flagged, they'll want to know why, in their language, in real time. When something is blocked, they'll expect a resolution path, not a wall. The platforms that win will be those that treat fraud prevention not as an internal function, but as a public experience, visible, thoughtful, and emotionally intelligent.

And behind all this, there will be people; the engineers, analysts, and decision-makers who keep these systems running. Their roles will shift. They won't just write code or review logs. They'll design models, audit decisions, mentor AI behavior, and architect for adaptation. Their superpower will not be expertise alone — it will be **discipline in uncertainty**, the ability to build systems that are strong, yet flexible. Secure, yet kind. Automated, yet accountable.

The future of secure software engineering won't just belong to the technically skilled, it will belong to those who can think across disciplines. As fraud threats become more algorithmic and detection systems more intelligent, the line between AI engineering and cybersecurity will continue to dissolve. Already, teams are shifting away from silos: instead of data scientists training models in isolation and security engineers plugging in alerts after deployment, there is now a push toward converged roles, hybrid professionals who understand both threat vectors and machine learning pipelines.

This convergence isn't a trend. It's a necessity. A fraud analyst who can't interpret model scores will miss subtle patterns. An AI engineer who can't understand social engineering techniques will underweight critical signals. And an operations lead who doesn't grasp compliance trade-offs may deploy a feature that violates regulatory frameworks. The most valuable professionals in the next decade will be those who can connect code, context, and consequence, those who can build systems that not only work, but work responsibly in a chaotic world.

One area that will gain even more importance is proactive threat modeling; a practice often associated with software security but increasingly necessary in fraud prevention. In the future, fraud systems will be tested before they're even deployed not just for performance, but for exploitability. Teams will simulate adversaries using AI-powered red-teaming tools, deliberately probing fraud models with adversarial inputs to see how they behave under pressure.

These simulations won't be reserved for incident response, they will become a routine part of engineering. Before a new feature goes live, before a model is retrained, before a customer flow is redesigned, fraud teams will sit with product teams and ask: "If you were trying to game this system, how would you do it?" And rather than react to those insights later, they'll embed countermeasures early, baking resilience into the very structure of software design.

This mindset shift, from reactive to proactive, from incident response to anticipatory architecture will define the most secure systems of the future. Because the strongest fraud defenses won't be those that catch fraud after it happens. They'll be the ones that make fraud too expensive, too slow, too unpredictable to scale.

But even the best systems are built by people and here lies one of the most pressing challenges of the next decade: talent. The demand for professionals who understand AI, security, software engineering, and compliance is already outpacing supply. And retaining that talent will take more than salaries or titles. It will require meaningful work, supportive cultures, and leadership that empowers ethical decisions.

Too often, security and fraud engineers are treated as blockers called in late, asked to say no, and blamed when systems break. But in tomorrow's world, these roles will be **drivers of innovation**, not constraints on it. Teams that give fraud engineers a seat at the product table, that celebrate responsible launches, that invest in upskilling, and that build psychologically safe environments for dissent, those teams will not only keep their talent. They will lead the industry.

In many ways, secure software engineering in finance is about fighting entropy. Systems drift. Users change. Attackers evolve. Teams shift. Regulations tighten. The work is never done. And that's the point. The job is not to "solve" fraud. It's to continually outlearn it. It's to build systems that respond with strength, repair with grace, and grow more resilient with every breach, every fix, every lesson.

## Designing for Disruption: Building for the Unknown

If the past decade has taught the tech world anything, it's that disruption is not a once-in-a-generation event, it's a recurring reality. Pandemics, wars, regulatory shifts, economic collapses, and geopolitical tension have all altered the rules of engagement for fintechs, banks, and security teams. The systems that survived didn't just scale. They absorbed change without falling apart.

In the next phase of secure software engineering, the most resilient systems will be those that assume everything can change. Threat surfaces will change. User behavior will shift. Infrastructure may be migrated across continents overnight. Regulatory policy may reverse years of product design. Even AI models, once trusted, may require complete re-engineering due to a single bias report or legal ruling.

To design for disruption means building modularity into every layer. Fraud detection models must be swappable. Risk scoring pipelines must be interruptible. Response protocols must be able to degrade gracefully without exposing the system. In other words, secure systems should be architected like resilient cities not rigid walls, but networks of flexible structures capable of absorbing pressure and evolving on demand.

The platforms that survive aren't just the ones that detect well. They're the ones that expect volatility and adapt with precision.

## Collaboration as Infrastructure: Why No Team Builds Alone

Fraud prevention is no longer a product feature. It is a shared responsibility. The days of siloed engineering and lone-wolf security teams are ending. As AI systems become more deeply embedded into finance, product, compliance, operations, legal, customer success, and even marketing must have a shared understanding of how these systems behave and how they respond under pressure.

This collaboration is not just cultural — it must be structured into the platform itself. Alert systems must surface relevant signals to relevant teams. Documentation must be searchable, version-controlled, and legible to non-engineers. Decision logs must be human-readable, not just machine traceable. And communication must be fast, accessible, and built into the daily rhythm of work.

In many high-performing teams, this collaboration takes the form of cross-functional fraud councils—groups that meet weekly to review trends, flag concerns, approve model updates, and stress-test mitigation strategies. Others embed fraud specialists inside product teams, ensuring that new features are reviewed in real time, not in postmortems.

This kind of coordination is no longer optional. Because in the next era, fraudsters will not exploit code alone, they will exploit organizational gaps. Delayed communication, unclear ownership, or mismatched expectations will become their playgrounds. And the best defense will be teams that think together, plan together, and act as one.

## Legacy and Leadership: Engineering Beyond the Codebase

At some point, every engineer, analyst, or decision-maker faces a deeper question: What will outlast me? In a field that moves fast, with tools evolving yearly and models becoming outdated within months, what remains? The answer, increasingly, is systems of thinking.

Codebases get rewritten. Platforms get acquired. But the way a team approaches fraud; the values, the discipline, the questions they ask before they launch, the assumptions they test before deployment, those create legacy. The best leaders don't just ship strong features. They create frameworks that others can build on safely, long after they're gone.

In the future of financial software, legacy will be defined not by innovation speed alone, but by the consistency of ethical judgment across scale. Leaders who design systems that protect everyone equally who enforce not just uptime but fairness, not just speed but traceability will leave behind organizations that do the right thing, even under pressure.

And the new generation of security engineers? They're not just technologists. They're philosophers. They ask: What assumptions are baked into our model? Who benefits from this design choice?

What are we not seeing? And in that way, they move the field forward not just through technology, but through thoughtful, human-first leadership.

Because in the end, every fraud defense, every AI decision, every secure transaction; it all comes back to people. The people who use the system. The people who build it. The people who believe in what it protects.

# About the Author

Gbenga Akingbulere is a globally respected software engineering leader and AI-powered cybersecurity architect, widely recognized for his pioneering work in developing secure, intelligent systems that power the backbone of modern financial infrastructures. With over a decade of hands-on experience, he sits at the intersection of artificial intelligence, cloud-native security, and software resilience, redefining how organizations detect, prevent, and respond to financial fraud at scale.

He began his career designing enterprise-grade applications in Lagos, where early exposure to the fast-paced world of digital payments revealed the fragility and complexity of financial security systems in emerging markets. From these foundational years, he developed not only the technical skillset required to build high-impact solutions, but also a personal philosophy rooted in clarity, integrity, and the belief that secure systems must protect people, not just processes.

His career has since expanded into a global footprint. His work at Ash Nelson Partners led to the creation of several AI-powered fraud detection systems, many of which now serve as blueprints for secure transaction flows in West Africa.

Beyond code, he is a teacher, reviewer, and active contributor to global security and AI communities. He has served on technical review boards, judged innovation in AI-driven software architecture, and spoken at fintech roundtables and developer events; always championing systems that are not only fast and scalable, but fair, explainable, and ethical.

His work reflects a rare blend of practical engineering excellence and forward-thinking strategic insight. Whether he's automating threat response, refining model pipelines, or guiding startups on secure-by-design principles, he brings a sense of purpose to every system he helps build. He believes the future of software lies in cross-functional thinking, disciplined risk mitigation, and teams that treat security not as an obstacle, but as an accelerant for trust.

He holds advanced certifications in cloud security, DevSecOps, and machine learning systems, but he values outcomes more than accolades. What matters most to him is real-world impact, whether it's reducing breach incidents for a fintech client, streamlining fraud investigations across a multi-region platform, or mentoring younger engineers in the art of responsible innovation.

Through this book, he shares not only frameworks and methodologies, but stories, insights, and lessons drawn from systems that worked and those that nearly failed. It is a culmination of lived experience, collaborative problem-solving, and relentless learning in the fast-moving world of financial security.

Today, he continues to build, write, and lead at the frontier of AI-powered secure software engineering, always with the same goal in mind: to help others build systems that are smart, secure, and built to last not just for users, but for the future.

Gbenga Akingbulere

# References


Anderson, R. (2020). Security Engineering: A Guide to Building Dependable Distributed Systems (3rd ed.). Wiley.

Arora, A., & Garg, R. (2021). Machine Learning for Cybersecurity: Foundations and Applications. Springer.

Basiron, M., et al. (2021). "AI-Driven Anomaly Detection in FinTech Platforms." Journal of Financial Cybersecurity, 12(3), 145–159.

Google Cloud. (2022). Security Foundations Blueprint. Retrieved from https://cloud.google.com/security

Microsoft. (2023). Responsible AI Standard: A Framework for Building Trustworthy AI. Retrieved from https://www.microsoft.com/responsible-ai

National Institute of Standards and Technology (NIST). (2023). AI Risk Management Framework (AI RMF 1.0). Retrieved from https://www.nist.gov/itl/ai-risk-management-framework

OWASP Foundation. (2023). OWASP Top 10 for Large Language Model Applications & Top 10 for Machine Learning Security. Retrieved from https://owasp.org

Sculley, D., et al. (2015). "Hidden Technical Debt in Machine Learning Systems." Advances in Neural Information Processing Systems (NeurIPS).

Stripe. (2022). Machine Learning in Fraud Prevention: Balancing Risk and User Experience. Retrieved from https://stripe.com/blog

Turing Institute. (2021). Ethics and Explainability in AI for Financial Services. Retrieved from https://www.turing.ac.uk

World Bank. (2022). The Evolution of Digital Financial Services in Africa: Cybersecurity Risks and Controls. Retrieved from https://worldbank.org

Zhang, K., & Chen, S. (2020). AI Security: Threats and Defense Strategies. Elsevier.

www.ingramcontent.com/pod-product-compliance
Lightning Source LLC
LaVergne TN
LVHW090857240726
843527LV00048B/13